OpenOCD - Open On-Chip Debugger Reference Manual

A catalogue record for this book is available from the Hong Kong Public Libraries.

Published in Hong Kong by Samurai Media Limited.

Email: info@samuraimedia.org

ISBN 978-988-8381-16-6

Background Cover Image by https://www.flickr.com/people/webtreatsetc/

Short Contents

Table of Contents

About

OpenOCD was created by Dominic Rath as part of a 2005 diploma thesis written at the University of Applied Sciences Augsburg (http://www.hs-augsburg.de). Since that time, the project has grown into an active open-source project, supported by a diverse community of software and hardware developers from around the world.

What is OpenOCD?

The Open On-Chip Debugger (OpenOCD) aims to provide debugging, in-system programming and boundary-scan testing for embedded target devices.

It does so with the assistance of a *debug adapter*, which is a small hardware module which helps provide the right kind of electrical signaling to the target being debugged. These are required since the debug host (on which OpenOCD runs) won't usually have native support for such signaling, or the connector needed to hook up to the target.

Such debug adapters support one or more *transport* protocols, each of which involves different electrical signaling (and uses different messaging protocols on top of that signaling). There are many types of debug adapter, and little uniformity in what they are called. (There are also product naming differences.)

These adapters are sometimes packaged as discrete dongles, which may generically be called *hardware interface dongles*. Some development boards also integrate them directly, which may let the development board connect directly to the debug host over USB (and sometimes also to power it over USB).

For example, a *JTAG Adapter* supports JTAG signaling, and is used to communicate with JTAG (IEEE 1149.1) compliant TAPs on your target board. A *TAP* is a "Test Access Port", a module which processes special instructions and data. TAPs are daisy-chained within and between chips and boards. JTAG supports debugging and boundary scan operations.

There are also *SWD Adapters* that support Serial Wire Debug (SWD) signaling to communicate with some newer ARM cores, as well as debug adapters which support both JTAG and SWD transports. SWD supports only debugging, whereas JTAG also supports boundary scan operations.

For some chips, there are also *Programming Adapters* supporting special transports used only to write code to flash memory, without support for on-chip debugging or boundary scan. (At this writing, OpenOCD does not support such non-debug adapters.)

Dongles: OpenOCD currently supports many types of hardware dongles: USB-based, parallel port-based, and other standalone boxes that run OpenOCD internally. See Chapter 2 [Debug Adapter Hardware], page 5.

GDB Debug: It allows ARM7 (ARM7TDMI and ARM720t), ARM9 (ARM920T, ARM922T, ARM926EJ–S, ARM966E–S), XScale (PXA25x, IXP42x), Cortex-M3 (Stellaris LM3, ST STM32 and Energy Micro EFM32) and Intel Quark (x10xx) based cores to be debugged via the GDB protocol.

Flash Programming: Flash writing is supported for external CFI-compatible NOR flashes (Intel and AMD/Spansion command set) and several internal flashes (LPC1700, LPC1800, LPC2000, LPC4300, AT91SAM7, AT91SAM3U, STR7x, STR9x, LM3, STM32x and EFM32). Preliminary support for various NAND flash controllers (LPC3180, Orion, S3C24xx, more) is included.

OpenOCD Web Site

The OpenOCD web site provides the latest public news from the community:

`http://openocd.org/`

Latest User's Guide:

The user's guide you are now reading may not be the latest one available. A version for more recent code may be available. Its HTML form is published regularly at:

`http://openocd.org/doc/html/index.html`

PDF form is likewise published at:

`http://openocd.org/doc/pdf/openocd.pdf`

OpenOCD User's Forum

There is an OpenOCD forum (phpBB) hosted by SparkFun, which might be helpful to you. Note that if you want anything to come to the attention of developers, you should post it to the OpenOCD Developer Mailing List instead of this forum.

`http://forum.sparkfun.com/viewforum.php?f=18`

OpenOCD User's Mailing List

The OpenOCD User Mailing List provides the primary means of communication between users:

`https://lists.sourceforge.net/mailman/listinfo/openocd-user`

OpenOCD IRC

Support can also be found on irc: `irc://irc.freenode.net/openocd`

1 OpenOCD Developer Resources

If you are interested in improving the state of OpenOCD's debugging and testing support, new contributions will be welcome. Motivated developers can produce new target, flash or interface drivers, improve the documentation, as well as more conventional bug fixes and enhancements.

The resources in this chapter are available for developers wishing to explore or expand the OpenOCD source code.

1.1 OpenOCD Git Repository

During the 0.3.x release cycle, OpenOCD switched from Subversion to a Git repository hosted at SourceForge. The repository URL is:

`git://git.code.sf.net/p/openocd/code`

or via http

`http://git.code.sf.net/p/openocd/code`

You may prefer to use a mirror and the HTTP protocol:

`http://repo.or.cz/r/openocd.git`

With standard Git tools, use `git clone` to initialize a local repository, and `git pull` to update it. There are also gitweb pages letting you browse the repository with a web browser, or download arbitrary snapshots without needing a Git client:

`http://repo.or.cz/w/openocd.git`

The `README` file contains the instructions for building the project from the repository or a snapshot.

Developers that want to contribute patches to the OpenOCD system are **strongly** encouraged to work against mainline. Patches created against older versions may require additional work from their submitter in order to be updated for newer releases.

1.2 Doxygen Developer Manual

During the 0.2.x release cycle, the OpenOCD project began providing a Doxygen reference manual. This document contains more technical information about the software internals, development processes, and similar documentation:

`http://openocd.org/doc/doxygen/html/index.html`

This document is a work-in-progress, but contributions would be welcome to fill in the gaps. All of the source files are provided in-tree, listed in the Doxyfile configuration at the top of the source tree.

1.3 Gerrit Review System

All changes in the OpenOCD Git repository go through the web-based Gerrit Code Review System:

`http://openocd.zylin.com/`

After a one-time registration and repository setup, anyone can push commits from their local Git repository directly into Gerrit. All users and developers are encouraged to review, test, discuss and vote for changes in Gerrit. The feedback provides the basis for a maintainer to eventually submit the change to the main Git repository.

The `HACKING` file, also available as the Patch Guide in the Doxygen Developer Manual, contains basic information about how to connect a repository to Gerrit, prepare and push patches. Patch authors are expected to maintain their changes while they're in Gerrit, respond to feedback and if necessary rework and push improved versions of the change.

1.4 OpenOCD Developer Mailing List

The OpenOCD Developer Mailing List provides the primary means of communication between developers:

`https://lists.sourceforge.net/mailman/listinfo/openocd-devel`

1.5 OpenOCD Bug Tracker

The OpenOCD Bug Tracker is hosted on SourceForge:

`http://bugs.openocd.org/`

2 Debug Adapter Hardware

Defined: **dongle**: A small device that plugs into a computer and serves as an adapter ....
[snip]

In the OpenOCD case, this generally refers to **a small adapter** that attaches to your computer via USB or the parallel port. One exception is the Ultimate Solutions ZY1000, packaged as a small box you attach via an ethernet cable. The ZY1000 has the advantage that it does not require any drivers to be installed on the developer PC. It also has a built in web interface. It supports RTCK/RCLK or adaptive clocking and has a built-in relay to power cycle targets remotely.

2.1 Choosing a Dongle

There are several things you should keep in mind when choosing a dongle.

1. **Transport** Does it support the kind of communication that you need? OpenOCD focusses mostly on JTAG. Your version may also support other ways to communicate with target devices.

2. **Voltage** What voltage is your target - 1.8, 2.8, 3.3, or 5V? Does your dongle support it? You might need a level converter.

3. **Pinout** What pinout does your target board use? Does your dongle support it? You may be able to use jumper wires, or an "octopus" connector, to convert pinouts.

4. **Connection** Does your computer have the USB, parallel, or Ethernet port needed?

5. **RTCK** Do you expect to use it with ARM chips and boards with RTCK support (also known as "adaptive clocking")?

2.2 Stand-alone JTAG Probe

The ZY1000 from Ultimate Solutions is technically not a dongle but a stand-alone JTAG probe that, unlike most dongles, doesn't require any drivers running on the developer's host computer. Once installed on a network using DHCP or a static IP assignment, users can access the ZY1000 probe locally or remotely from any host with access to the IP address assigned to the probe. The ZY1000 provides an intuitive web interface with direct access to the OpenOCD debugger. Users may also run a GDBSERVER directly on the ZY1000 to take full advantage of GCC & GDB to debug any distribution of embedded Linux or NetBSD running on the target. The ZY1000 supports RTCK & RCLK or adaptive clocking and has a built-in relay to power cycle the target remotely.

For more information, visit:

ZY1000 See: `http://www.ultsol.com/index.php/component/content/article/8/210-zylin-zy1000-main`

2.3 USB FT2232 Based

There are many USB JTAG dongles on the market, many of them based on a chip from "Future Technology Devices International" (FTDI) known as the FTDI FT2232; this is a USB full speed (12 Mbps) chip. See: `http://www.ftdichip.com` for more information. In summer 2009, USB high speed (480 Mbps) versions of these FTDI chips started to become available in JTAG adapters. Around 2012, a new variant appeared - FT232H - this is a single-channel version of FT2232H. (Adapters using those high speed FT2232H or FT232H chips may support adaptive clocking.)

The FT2232 chips are flexible enough to support some other transport options, such as SWD or the SPI variants used to program some chips. They have two communications channels, and one can be used for a UART adapter at the same time the other one is used to provide a debug adapter.

Also, some development boards integrate an FT2232 chip to serve as a built-in low-cost debug adapter and USB-to-serial solution.

- **usbjtag**
  Link `http://elk.informatik.fh-augsburg.de/hhweb/doc/openocd/usbjtag/usbjtag.html`

- **jtagkey**
  See: `http://www.amontec.com/jtagkey.shtml`

- **jtagkey2**
  See: `http://www.amontec.com/jtagkey2.shtml`

- **oocdlink**
  See: `http://www.oocdlink.com` By Joern Kaipf

- **signalyzer**
  See: `http://www.signalyzer.com`

- **Stellaris Eval Boards**
  See: `http://www.ti.com` - The Stellaris eval boards bundle FT2232-based JTAG and SWD support, which can be used to debug the Stellaris chips. Using separate JTAG adapters is optional. These boards can also be used in a "pass through" mode as JTAG adapters to other target boards, disabling the Stellaris chip.

- **TI/Luminary ICDI**
  See: `http://www.ti.com` - TI/Luminary In-Circuit Debug Interface (ICDI) Boards are included in Stellaris LM3S9B9x Evaluation Kits. Like the non-detachable FT2232 support on the other Stellaris eval boards, they can be used to debug other target boards.

- **olimex-jtag**
  See: `http://www.olimex.com`

- **Flyswatter/Flyswatter2**
  See: `http://www.tincantools.com`

- **turtelizer2**
  See: Turtelizer 2, or `http://www.ethernut.de`

- **comstick**
  Link: `http://www.hitex.com/index.php?id=383`

- **stm32stick**
  Link `http://www.hitex.com/stm32-stick`

- **axm0432_jtag**
  Axiom AXM-0432 Link `http://www.axman.com` - NOTE: This JTAG does not appear to be available anymore as of April 2012.

- **cortino**
  Link `http://www.hitex.com/index.php?id=cortino`
- **dlp-usb1232h**
  Link `http://www.dlpdesign.com/usb/usb1232h.shtml`
- **digilent-hs1**
  Link `http://www.digilentinc.com/Products/Detail.cfm?Prod=JTAG-HS1`
- **opendous**
  Link `http://code.google.com/p/opendous/wiki/JTAG` FT2232H-based (OpenHardware).
- **JTAG-lock-pick Tiny 2**
  Link `http://www.distortec.com/jtag-lock-pick-tiny-2` FT232H-based
- **GW16042**
  Link: `http://shop.gateworks.com/index.php?route=product/product&path=70_80&product_id=64` FT2232H-based

2.4 USB-JTAG / Altera USB-Blaster compatibles

These devices also show up as FTDI devices, but are not protocol-compatible with the FT2232 devices. They are, however, protocol-compatible among themselves. USB-JTAG devices typically consist of a FT245 followed by a CPLD that understands a particular protocol, or emulates this protocol using some other hardware.

They may appear under different USB VID/PID depending on the particular product. The driver can be configured to search for any VID/PID pair (see the section on driver commands).

- **USB-JTAG** Kolja Waschk's USB Blaster-compatible adapter
  Link: `http://ixo-jtag.sourceforge.net/`
- **Altera USB-Blaster**
  Link: `http://www.altera.com/literature/ug/ug_usb_blstr.pdf`

2.5 USB JLINK based

There are several OEM versions of the Segger **JLINK** adapter. It is an example of a micro controller based JTAG adapter, it uses an AT91SAM764 internally.

- **ATMEL SAMICE** Only works with ATMEL chips!
  Link: `http://www.atmel.com/dyn/products/tools_card.asp?tool_id=3892`
- **SEGGER JLINK**
  Link: `http://www.segger.com/jlink.html`
- **IAR J-Link**
  Link: `http://www.iar.com/en/products/hardware-debug-probes/iar-j-link/`

2.6 USB RLINK based

Raisonance has an adapter called **RLink**. It exists in a stripped-down form on the STM32 Primer, permanently attached to the JTAG lines. It also exists on the STM32 Primer2, but that is wired for SWD and not JTAG, thus not supported.

- **Raisonance RLink**
  Link: `http: / / www . mcu-raisonance . com / ~rlink-debugger-programmer__ microcontrollers__tool~tool__T018:4cn9ziz4bnx6.html`
- **STM32 Primer**
  Link: `http://www.stm32circle.com/resources/stm32primer.php`
- **STM32 Primer2**
  Link: `http://www.stm32circle.com/resources/stm32primer2.php`

2.7 USB ST-LINK based

ST Micro has an adapter called **ST-LINK**. They only work with ST Micro chips, notably STM32 and STM8.

- **ST-LINK**
  This is available standalone and as part of some kits, eg. STM32VLDISCOVERY.
  Link: `http://www.st.com/internet/evalboard/product/219866.jsp`
- **ST-LINK/V2**
  This is available standalone and as part of some kits, eg. STM32F4DISCOVERY.
  Link: `http://www.st.com/internet/evalboard/product/251168.jsp`

For info the original ST-LINK enumerates using the mass storage usb class; however, its implementation is completely broken. The result is this causes issues under Linux. The simplest solution is to get Linux to ignore the ST-LINK using one of the following methods:

- modprobe -r usb-storage && modprobe usb-storage quirks=483:3744:i
- add "options usb-storage quirks=483:3744:i" to /etc/modprobe.conf

2.8 USB TI/Stellaris ICDI based

Texas Instruments has an adapter called **ICDI**. It is not to be confused with the FTDI based adapters that were originally fitted to their evaluation boards. This is the adapter fitted to the Stellaris LaunchPad.

2.9 USB CMSIS-DAP based

ARM has released a interface standard called CMSIS-DAP that simplifies connecting debuggers to ARM Cortex based targets `http://www.keil.com/support/man/docs/dapdebug/ dapdebug_introduction.htm`.

2.10 USB Other

- **USBprog**
  Link: `http://shop.embedded-projects.net/` - which uses an Atmel MEGA32 and a UBN9604
- **USB - Presto**
  Link: `http://tools.asix.net/prg_presto.htm`
- **Versaloon-Link**
  Link: `http://www.versaloon.com`
- **ARM-JTAG-EW**
  Link: `http://www.olimex.com/dev/arm-jtag-ew.html`

- **Buspirate**
  Link: `http://dangerousprototypes.com/bus-pirate-manual/`
- **opendous**
  Link: `http://code.google.com/p/opendous-jtag/` - which uses an AT90USB162
- **estick**
  Link: `http://code.google.com/p/estick-jtag/`
- **Keil ULINK v1**
  Link: `http://www.keil.com/ulink1/`

2.11 IBM PC Parallel Printer Port Based

The two well-known "JTAG Parallel Ports" cables are the Xilinx DLC5 and the Macraigor Wiggler. There are many clones and variations of these on the market.

Note that parallel ports are becoming much less common, so if you have the choice you should probably avoid these adapters in favor of USB-based ones.

- **Wiggler** - There are many clones of this.
  Link: `http://www.macraigor.com/wiggler.htm`
- **DLC5** - From XILINX - There are many clones of this
  Link: Search the web for: "XILINX DLC5" - it is no longer produced, PDF schematics are easily found and it is easy to make.
- **Amontec - JTAG Accelerator**
  Link: `http://www.amontec.com/jtag_accelerator.shtml`
- **Wiggler2**
  Link: `http://www.ccac.rwth-aachen.de/~michaels/index.php/hardware/armjtag`
- **Wiggler_ntrst_inverted**
  Yet another variation - See the source code, src/jtag/parport.c
- **old_amt_wiggler**
  Unknown - probably not on the market today
- **arm-jtag**
  Link: Most likely `http://www.olimex.com/dev/arm-jtag.html` [another wiggler clone]
- **chameleon**
  Link: `http://www.amontec.com/chameleon.shtml`
- **Triton**
  Unknown.
- **Lattice**
  ispDownload from Lattice Semiconductor `http://www.latticesemi.com/lit/docs/devtools/dlcable.pdf`
- **flashlink**
  From ST Microsystems;
  Link: `http://www.st.com/internet/com/TECHNICAL_RESOURCES/TECHNICAL_LITERATURE/DATA_BRIEF/DM00039500.pdf`

2.12 Other...

- **ep93xx**
  An EP93xx based Linux machine using the GPIO pins directly.

- **at91rm9200**
  Like the EP93xx - but an ATMEL AT91RM9200 based solution using the GPIO pins on the chip.

- **bcm2835gpio**
  A BCM2835-based board (e.g. Raspberry Pi) using the GPIO pins of the expansion header.

- **jtag_vpi**
  A JTAG driver acting as a client for the JTAG VPI server interface.
  Link: `http://github.com/fjullien/jtag_vpi`

3 About Jim-Tcl

OpenOCD uses a small "Tcl Interpreter" known as Jim-Tcl. This programming language provides a simple and extensible command interpreter.

All commands presented in this Guide are extensions to Jim-Tcl. You can use them as simple commands, without needing to learn much of anything about Tcl. Alternatively, you can write Tcl programs with them.

You can learn more about Jim at its website, `http://jim.tcl.tk`. There is an active and responsive community, get on the mailing list if you have any questions. Jim-Tcl maintainers also lurk on the OpenOCD mailing list.

- **Jim vs. Tcl**
  Jim-Tcl is a stripped down version of the well known Tcl language, which can be found here: `http://www.tcl.tk`. Jim-Tcl has far fewer features. Jim-Tcl is several dozens of .C files and .H files and implements the basic Tcl command set. In contrast: Tcl 8.6 is a 4.2 MB .zip file containing 1540 files.

- **Missing Features**
  Our practice has been: Add/clone the real Tcl feature if/when needed. We welcome Jim-Tcl improvements, not bloat. Also there are a large number of optional Jim-Tcl features that are not enabled in OpenOCD.

- **Scripts**
  OpenOCD configuration scripts are Jim-Tcl Scripts. OpenOCD's command interpreter today is a mixture of (newer) Jim-Tcl commands, and the (older) original command interpreter.

- **Commands**
  At the OpenOCD telnet command line (or via the GDB monitor command) one can type a Tcl for() loop, set variables, etc. Some of the commands documented in this guide are implemented as Tcl scripts, from a `startup.tcl` file internal to the server.

- **Historical Note**
  Jim-Tcl was introduced to OpenOCD in spring 2008. Fall 2010, before OpenOCD 0.5 release, OpenOCD switched to using Jim-Tcl as a Git submodule, which greatly simplified upgrading Jim-Tcl to benefit from new features and bugfixes in Jim-Tcl.

- **Need a crash course in Tcl?**
  See Chapter 24 [Tcl Crash Course], page 138.

4 Running

Properly installing OpenOCD sets up your operating system to grant it access to the debug adapters. On Linux, this usually involves installing a file in **/etc/udev/rules.d**, so OpenOCD has permissions. An example rules file that works for many common adapters is shipped with OpenOCD in the **contrib** directory. MS-Windows needs complex and confusing driver configuration for every peripheral. Such issues are unique to each operating system, and are not detailed in this User's Guide.

Then later you will invoke the OpenOCD server, with various options to tell it how each debug session should work. The **--help** option shows:

```
bash$ openocd --help
```

```
--help       | -h        display this help
--version    | -v        display OpenOCD version
--file       | -f        use configuration file <name>
--search     | -s        dir to search for config files and scripts
--debug      | -d        set debug level <0-3>
--log_output | -l        redirect log output to file <name>
--command    | -c        run <command>
```

If you don't give any **-f** or **-c** options, OpenOCD tries to read the configuration file **openocd.cfg**. To specify one or more different configuration files, use **-f** options. For example:

```
openocd -f config1.cfg -f config2.cfg -f config3.cfg
```

Configuration files and scripts are searched for in

1. the current directory,
2. any search dir specified on the command line using the **-s** option,
3. any search dir specified using the **add_script_search_dir** command,
4. **$HOME/.openocd** (not on Windows),
5. the site wide script library **$pkgdatadir/site** and
6. the OpenOCD-supplied script library **$pkgdatadir/scripts**.

The first found file with a matching file name will be used.

> **Note:** Don't try to use configuration script names or paths which include the "#" character. That character begins Tcl comments.

4.1 Simple setup, no customization

In the best case, you can use two scripts from one of the script libraries, hook up your JTAG adapter, and start the server ... and your JTAG setup will just work "out of the box". Always try to start by reusing those scripts, but assume you'll need more customization even if this works. See Chapter 5 [OpenOCD Project Setup], page 14.

If you find a script for your JTAG adapter, and for your board or target, you may be able to hook up your JTAG adapter then start the server with some variation of one of the following:

```
openocd -f interface/ADAPTER.cfg -f board/MYBOARD.cfg
openocd -f interface/ftdi/ADAPTER.cfg -f board/MYBOARD.cfg
```

You might also need to configure which reset signals are present, using `-c 'reset_config trst_and_srst'` or something similar. If all goes well you'll see output something like

```
Open On-Chip Debugger 0.4.0 (2010-01-14-15:06)
For bug reports, read
        http://openocd.org/doc/doxygen/bugs.html
Info : JTAG tap: lm3s.cpu tap/device found: 0x3ba00477
        (mfg: 0x23b, part: 0xba00, ver: 0x3)
```

Seeing that "tap/device found" message, and no warnings, means the JTAG communication is working. That's a key milestone, but you'll probably need more project-specific setup.

4.2 What OpenOCD does as it starts

OpenOCD starts by processing the configuration commands provided on the command line or, if there were no `-c command` or `-f file.cfg` options given, in `openocd.cfg`. See [Configuration Stage], page 32. At the end of the configuration stage it verifies the JTAG scan chain defined using those commands; your configuration should ensure that this always succeeds. Normally, OpenOCD then starts running as a daemon. Alternatively, commands may be used to terminate the configuration stage early, perform work (such as updating some flash memory), and then shut down without acting as a daemon.

Once OpenOCD starts running as a daemon, it waits for connections from clients (Telnet, GDB, Other) and processes the commands issued through those channels.

If you are having problems, you can enable internal debug messages via the `-d` option.

Also it is possible to interleave Jim-Tcl commands w/config scripts using the `-c` command line switch.

To enable debug output (when reporting problems or working on OpenOCD itself), use the `-d` command line switch. This sets the `debug_level` to "3", outputting the most information, including debug messages. The default setting is "2", outputting only informational messages, warnings and errors. You can also change this setting from within a telnet or gdb session using `debug_level<n>` (see [debug_level], page 96).

You can redirect all output from the daemon to a file using the `-l <logfile>` switch.

Note! OpenOCD will launch the GDB & telnet server even if it can not establish a connection with the target. In general, it is possible for the JTAG controller to be unresponsive until the target is set up correctly via e.g. GDB monitor commands in a GDB init script.

5 OpenOCD Project Setup

To use OpenOCD with your development projects, you need to do more than just connect the JTAG adapter hardware (dongle) to your development board and start the OpenOCD server. You also need to configure your OpenOCD server so that it knows about your adapter and board, and helps your work. You may also want to connect OpenOCD to GDB, possibly using Eclipse or some other GUI.

5.1 Hooking up the JTAG Adapter

Today's most common case is a dongle with a JTAG cable on one side (such as a ribbon cable with a 10-pin or 20-pin IDC connector) and a USB cable on the other. Instead of USB, some cables use Ethernet; older ones may use a PC parallel port, or even a serial port.

1. *Start with power to your target board turned off*, and nothing connected to your JTAG adapter. If you're particularly paranoid, unplug power to the board. It's important to have the ground signal properly set up, unless you are using a JTAG adapter which provides galvanic isolation between the target board and the debugging host.

2. *Be sure it's the right kind of JTAG connector.* If your dongle has a 20-pin ARM connector, you need some kind of adapter (or octopus, see below) to hook it up to boards using 14-pin or 10-pin connectors ... or to 20-pin connectors which don't use ARM's pinout.

   In the same vein, make sure the voltage levels are compatible. Not all JTAG adapters have the level shifters needed to work with 1.2 Volt boards.

3. *Be certain the cable is properly oriented* or you might damage your board. In most cases there are only two possible ways to connect the cable. Connect the JTAG cable from your adapter to the board. Be sure it's firmly connected.

   In the best case, the connector is keyed to physically prevent you from inserting it wrong. This is most often done using a slot on the board's male connector housing, which must match a key on the JTAG cable's female connector. If there's no housing, then you must look carefully and make sure pin 1 on the cable hooks up to pin 1 on the board. Ribbon cables are frequently all grey except for a wire on one edge, which is red. The red wire is pin 1.

   Sometimes dongles provide cables where one end is an "octopus" of color coded single-wire connectors, instead of a connector block. These are great when converting from one JTAG pinout to another, but are tedious to set up. Use these with connector pinout diagrams to help you match up the adapter signals to the right board pins.

4. *Connect the adapter's other end* once the JTAG cable is connected. A USB, parallel, or serial port connector will go to the host which you are using to run OpenOCD. For Ethernet, consult the documentation and your network administrator.

   For USB-based JTAG adapters you have an easy sanity check at this point: does the host operating system see the JTAG adapter? If you're running Linux, try the `lsusb` command. If that host is an MS-Windows host, you'll need to install a driver before OpenOCD works.

5. *Connect the adapter's power supply, if needed.* This step is primarily for non-USB adapters, but sometimes USB adapters need extra power.

6. *Power up the target board.* Unless you just let the magic smoke escape, you're now ready to set up the OpenOCD server so you can use JTAG to work with that board.

Talk with the OpenOCD server using telnet (`telnet localhost 4444` on many systems) or GDB. See Chapter 21 [GDB and OpenOCD], page 125.

5.2 Project Directory

There are many ways you can configure OpenOCD and start it up.

A simple way to organize them all involves keeping a single directory for your work with a given board. When you start OpenOCD from that directory, it searches there first for configuration files, scripts, files accessed through semihosting, and for code you upload to the target board. It is also the natural place to write files, such as log files and data you download from the board.

5.3 Configuration Basics

There are two basic ways of configuring OpenOCD, and a variety of ways you can mix them. Think of the difference as just being how you start the server:

- Many `-f file` or `-c command` options on the command line
- No options, but a *user config file* in the current directory named `openocd.cfg`

Here is an example `openocd.cfg` file for a setup using a Signalyzer FT2232-based JTAG adapter to talk to a board with an Atmel AT91SAM7X256 microcontroller:

```
source [find interface/signalyzer.cfg]

# GDB can also flash my flash!
gdb_memory_map enable
gdb_flash_program enable

source [find target/sam7x256.cfg]
```

Here is the command line equivalent of that configuration:

```
openocd -f interface/signalyzer.cfg \
        -c "gdb_memory_map enable" \
        -c "gdb_flash_program enable" \
        -f target/sam7x256.cfg
```

You could wrap such long command lines in shell scripts, each supporting a different development task. One might re-flash the board with a specific firmware version. Another might set up a particular debugging or run-time environment.

> **Important:** At this writing (October 2009) the command line method has problems with how it treats variables. For example, after `-c "set VAR value"`, or doing the same in a script, the variable *VAR* will have no value that can be tested in a later script.

Here we will focus on the simpler solution: one user config file, including basic configuration plus any TCL procedures to simplify your work.

5.4 User Config Files

A user configuration file ties together all the parts of a project in one place. One of the
following will match your situation best:

- Ideally almost everything comes from configuration files provided by someone
  else. For example, OpenOCD distributes a `scripts` directory (probably in
  `/usr/share/openocd/scripts` on Linux). Board and tool vendors can provide these
  too, as can individual user sites; the `-s` command line option lets you say where to
  find these files. (See Chapter 4 [Running], page 12.) The AT91SAM7X256 example
  above works this way.

  Three main types of non-user configuration file each have their own subdirectory in the
  `scripts` directory:

  1. **interface** – one for each different debug adapter;
  2. **board** – one for each different board
  3. **target** – the chips which integrate CPUs and other JTAG TAPs

  Best case: include just two files, and they handle everything else. The first is an
  interface config file. The second is board-specific, and it sets up the JTAG TAPs and
  their GDB targets (by deferring to some `target.cfg` file), declares all flash memory,
  and leaves you nothing to do except meet your deadline:

  ```
  source [find interface/olimex-jtag-tiny.cfg]
  source [find board/csb337.cfg]
  ```

  Boards with a single microcontroller often won't need more than the target config file,
  as in the AT91SAM7X256 example. That's because there is no external memory (flash,
  DDR RAM), and the board differences are encapsulated by application code.

- Maybe you don't know yet what your board looks like to JTAG. Once you know the
  `interface.cfg` file to use, you may need help from OpenOCD to discover what's on the
  board. Once you find the JTAG TAPs, you can just search for appropriate target and
  board configuration files ... or write your own, from the bottom up. See [Autoprobing],
  page 59.

- You can often reuse some standard config files but need to write a few new ones,
  probably a `board.cfg` file. You will be using commands described later in this User's
  Guide, and working with the guidelines in the next chapter.

  For example, there may be configuration files for your JTAG adapter and target chip,
  but you need a new board-specific config file giving access to your particular flash chips.
  Or you might need to write another target chip configuration file for a new chip built
  around the Cortex M3 core.

  > **Note:** When you write new configuration files, please submit them for inclu-
  > sion in the next OpenOCD release. For example, a `board/newboard.cfg`
  > file will help the next users of that board, and a `target/newcpu.cfg` will
  > help support users of any board using that chip.

- You may may need to write some C code. It may be as simple as supporting a new
  FT2232 or parport based adapter; a bit more involved, like a NAND or NOR flash
  controller driver; or a big piece of work like supporting a new chip architecture.

Reuse the existing config files when you can. Look first in the `scripts/boards` area, then
`scripts/targets`. You may find a board configuration that's a good example to follow.

When you write config files, separate the reusable parts (things every user of that interface, chip, or board needs) from ones specific to your environment and debugging approach.

- For example, a `gdb-attach` event handler that invokes the `reset init` command will interfere with debugging early boot code, which performs some of the same actions that the `reset-init` event handler does.

- Likewise, the `arm9 vector_catch` command (or its siblings `xscale vector_catch` and `cortex_m vector_catch`) can be a timesaver during some debug sessions, but don't make everyone use that either. Keep those kinds of debugging aids in your user config file, along with messaging and tracing setup. (See [Software Debug Messages and Tracing], page 117.)

- You might need to override some defaults. For example, you might need to move, shrink, or back up the target's work area if your application needs much SRAM.

- TCP/IP port configuration is another example of something which is environment-specific, and should only appear in a user config file. See [TCP/IP Ports], page 33.

5.5 Project-Specific Utilities

A few project-specific utility routines may well speed up your work. Write them, and keep them in your project's user config file.

For example, if you are making a boot loader work on a board, it's nice to be able to debug the "after it's loaded to RAM" parts separately from the finicky early code which sets up the DDR RAM controller and clocks. A script like this one, or a more GDB-aware sibling, may help:

```
proc ramboot { } {
    # Reset, running the target's "reset-init" scripts
    # to initialize clocks and the DDR RAM controller.
    # Leave the CPU halted.
    reset init

    # Load CONFIG_SKIP_LOWLEVEL_INIT version into DDR RAM.
    load_image u-boot.bin 0x20000000

    # Start running.
    resume 0x20000000
}
```

Then once that code is working you will need to make it boot from NOR flash; a different utility would help. Alternatively, some developers write to flash using GDB. (You might use a similar script if you're working with a flash based microcontroller application instead of a boot loader.)

```
proc newboot { } {
    # Reset, leaving the CPU halted. The "reset-init" event
    # proc gives faster access to the CPU and to NOR flash;
    # "reset halt" would be slower.
    reset init
```

```
# Write standard version of U-Boot into the first two
# sectors of NOR flash ... the standard version should
# do the same lowlevel init as "reset-init".
flash protect 0 0 1 off
flash erase_sector 0 0 1
flash write_bank 0 u-boot.bin 0x0
flash protect 0 0 1 on

# Reboot from scratch using that new boot loader.
reset run
}
```

You may need more complicated utility procedures when booting from NAND. That often involves an extra bootloader stage, running from on-chip SRAM to perform DDR RAM setup so it can load the main bootloader code (which won't fit into that SRAM).

Other helper scripts might be used to write production system images, involving considerably more than just a three stage bootloader.

5.6 Target Software Changes

Sometimes you may want to make some small changes to the software you're developing, to help make JTAG debugging work better. For example, in C or assembly language code you might use #ifdef JTAG_DEBUG (or its converse) around code handling issues like:

- **Watchdog Timers**... Watchog timers are typically used to automatically reset systems if some application task doesn't periodically reset the timer. (The assumption is that the system has locked up if the task can't run.) When a JTAG debugger halts the system, that task won't be able to run and reset the timer ... potentially causing resets in the middle of your debug sessions.

  It's rarely a good idea to disable such watchdogs, since their usage needs to be debugged just like all other parts of your firmware. That might however be your only option.

  Look instead for chip-specific ways to stop the watchdog from counting while the system is in a debug halt state. It may be simplest to set that non-counting mode in your debugger startup scripts. You may however need a different approach when, for example, a motor could be physically damaged by firmware remaining inactive in a debug halt state. That might involve a type of firmware mode where that "non-counting" mode is disabled at the beginning then re-enabled at the end; a watchdog reset might fire and complicate the debug session, but hardware (or people) would be protected.[1]

- **ARM Semihosting**... When linked with a special runtime library provided with many toolchains[2], your target code can use I/O facilities on the debug host. That library provides a small set of system calls which are handled by OpenOCD. It can let the debugger provide your system console and a file system, helping with early debugging

---

[1] Note that many systems support a "monitor mode" debug that is a somewhat cleaner way to address such issues. You can think of it as only halting part of the system, maybe just one task, instead of the whole thing. At this writing, January 2010, OpenOCD based debugging does not support monitor mode debug, only "halt mode" debug.

[2] See chapter 8 "Semihosting" in ARM DUI 0203I, the "RealView Compilation Tools Developer Guide". The CodeSourcery EABI toolchain also includes a semihosting library.

or providing a more capable environment for sometimes-complex tasks like installing system firmware onto NAND or SPI flash.

- **ARM Wait-For-Interrupt**... Many ARM chips synchronize the JTAG clock using the core clock. Low power states which stop that core clock thus prevent JTAG access. Idle loops in tasking environments often enter those low power states via the `WFI` instruction (or its coprocessor equivalent, before ARMv7).

  You may want to *disable that instruction* in source code, or otherwise prevent using that state, to ensure you can get JTAG access at any time.[3] For example, the OpenOCD `halt` command may not work for an idle processor otherwise.

- **Delay after reset**... Not all chips have good support for debugger access right after reset; many LPC2xxx chips have issues here. Similarly, applications that reconfigure pins used for JTAG access as they start will also block debugger access.

  To work with boards like this, *enable a short delay loop* the first thing after reset, before "real" startup activities. For example, one second's delay is usually more than enough time for a JTAG debugger to attach, so that early code execution can be debugged or firmware can be replaced.

- **Debug Communications Channel (DCC)**... Some processors include mechanisms to send messages over JTAG. Many ARM cores support these, as do some cores from other vendors. (OpenOCD may be able to use this DCC internally, speeding up some operations like writing to memory.)

  Your application may want to deliver various debugging messages over JTAG, by *linking with a small library of code* provided with OpenOCD and using the utilities there to send various kinds of message. See [Software Debug Messages and Tracing], page 117.

5.7 Target Hardware Setup

Chip vendors often provide software development boards which are highly configurable, so that they can support all options that product boards may require. *Make sure that any jumpers or switches match the system configuration you are working with.*

Common issues include:

- **JTAG setup** ... Boards may support more than one JTAG configuration. Examples include jumpers controlling pullups versus pulldowns on the nTRST and/or nSRST signals, and choice of connectors (e.g. which of two headers on the base board, or one from a daughtercard). For some Texas Instruments boards, you may need to jumper the EMU0 and EMU1 signals (which OpenOCD won't currently control).

- **Boot Modes** ... Complex chips often support multiple boot modes, controlled by external jumpers. Make sure this is set up correctly. For example many i.MX boards from NXP need to be jumpered to "ATX mode" to start booting using the on-chip ROM, when using second stage bootloader code stored in a NAND flash chip.

  Such explicit configuration is common, and not limited to booting from NAND. You might also need to set jumpers to start booting using code loaded from an MMC/SD

---

[3] As a more polite alternative, some processors have special debug-oriented registers which can be used to change various features including how the low power states are clocked while debugging. The STM32 DBGMCU_CR register is an example; at the cost of extra power consumption, JTAG can be used during low power states.

card; external SPI flash; Ethernet, UART, or USB links; NOR flash; OneNAND flash; some external host; or various other sources.

- **Memory Addressing** ... Boards which support multiple boot modes may also have jumpers to configure memory addressing. One board, for example, jumpers external chipselect 0 (used for booting) to address either a large SRAM (which must be pre-loaded via JTAG), NOR flash, or NAND flash. When it's jumpered to address NAND flash, that board must also be told to start booting from on-chip ROM.

  Your `board.cfg` file may also need to be told this jumper configuration, so that it can know whether to declare NOR flash using `flash bank` or instead declare NAND flash with `nand device`; and likewise which probe to perform in its `reset-init` handler.

  A closely related issue is bus width. Jumpers might need to distinguish between 8 bit or 16 bit bus access for the flash used to start booting.

- **Peripheral Access** ... Development boards generally provide access to every peripheral on the chip, sometimes in multiple modes (such as by providing multiple audio codec chips). This interacts with software configuration of pin multiplexing, where for example a given pin may be routed either to the MMC/SD controller or the GPIO controller. It also often interacts with configuration jumpers. One jumper may be used to route signals to an MMC/SD card slot or an expansion bus (which might in turn affect booting); others might control which audio or video codecs are used.

Plus you should of course have `reset-init` event handlers which set up the hardware to match that jumper configuration. That includes in particular any oscillator or PLL used to clock the CPU, and any memory controllers needed to access external memory and peripherals. Without such handlers, you won't be able to access those resources without working target firmware which can do that setup ... this can be awkward when you're trying to debug that target firmware. Even if there's a ROM bootloader which handles a few issues, it rarely provides full access to all board-specific capabilities.

6 Config File Guidelines

This chapter is aimed at any user who needs to write a config file, including developers and integrators of OpenOCD and any user who needs to get a new board working smoothly. It provides guidelines for creating those files.

You should find the following directories under `$(INSTALLDIR)/scripts`, with config files maintained upstream. Use them as-is where you can; or as models for new files.

- `interface` ... These are for debug adapters. Files that specify configuration to use specific JTAG, SWD and other adapters go here.

- `board` ... Think Circuit Board, PWA, PCB, they go by many names. Board files contain initialization items that are specific to a board.

  They reuse target configuration files, since the same microprocessor chips are used on many boards, but support for external parts varies widely. For example, the SDRAM initialization sequence for the board, or the type of external flash and what address it uses. Any initialization sequence to enable that external flash or SDRAM should be found in the board file. Boards may also contain multiple targets: two CPUs; or a CPU and an FPGA.

- `target` ... Think chip. The "target" directory represents the JTAG TAPs on a chip which OpenOCD should control, not a board. Two common types of targets are ARM chips and FPGA or CPLD chips. When a chip has multiple TAPs (maybe it has both ARM and DSP cores), the target config file defines all of them.

- *more* ... browse for other library files which may be useful. For example, there are various generic and CPU-specific utilities.

The `openocd.cfg` user config file may override features in any of the above files by setting variables before sourcing the target file, or by adding commands specific to their situation.

6.1 Interface Config Files

The user config file should be able to source one of these files with a command like this:

    source [find interface/FOOBAR.cfg]

A preconfigured interface file should exist for every debug adapter in use today with OpenOCD. That said, perhaps some of these config files have only been used by the developer who created it.

A separate chapter gives information about how to set these up. See Chapter 8 [Debug Adapter Configuration], page 36. Read the OpenOCD source code (and Developer's Guide) if you have a new kind of hardware interface and need to provide a driver for it.

6.2 Board Config Files

The user config file should be able to source one of these files with a command like this:

    source [find board/FOOBAR.cfg]

The point of a board config file is to package everything about a given board that user config files need to know. In summary the board files should contain (if present)

1. One or more **source [find target/...cfg]** statements

2. NOR flash configuration (see [NOR Configuration], page 69)

3. NAND flash configuration (see [NAND Configuration], page 87)

4. Target **reset** handlers for SDRAM and I/O configuration

5. JTAG adapter reset configuration (see Chapter 9 [Reset Configuration], page 50)

6. All things that are not "inside a chip"

Generic things inside target chips belong in target config files, not board config files. So for example a **reset-init** event handler should know board-specific oscillator and PLL parameters, which it passes to target-specific utility code.

The most complex task of a board config file is creating such a **reset-init** event handler. Define those handlers last, after you verify the rest of the board configuration works.

6.2.1 Communication Between Config files

In addition to target-specific utility code, another way that board and target config files communicate is by following a convention on how to use certain variables.

The full Tcl/Tk language supports "namespaces", but Jim-Tcl does not. Thus the rule we follow in OpenOCD is this: Variables that begin with a leading underscore are temporary in nature, and can be modified and used at will within a target configuration file.

Complex board config files can do the things like this, for a board with three chips:

```
# Chip #1: PXA270 for network side, big endian
set CHIPNAME network
set ENDIAN big
source [find target/pxa270.cfg]
# on return: _TARGETNAME = network.cpu
# other commands can refer to the "network.cpu" target.
$_TARGETNAME configure .... events for this CPU..

# Chip #2: PXA270 for video side, little endian
set CHIPNAME video
set ENDIAN little
source [find target/pxa270.cfg]
# on return: _TARGETNAME = video.cpu
# other commands can refer to the "video.cpu" target.
$_TARGETNAME configure .... events for this CPU..

# Chip #3: Xilinx FPGA for glue logic
set CHIPNAME xilinx
unset ENDIAN
source [find target/spartan3.cfg]
```

That example is oversimplified because it doesn't show any flash memory, or the **reset-init** event handlers to initialize external DRAM or (assuming it needs it) load a configuration into the FPGA. Such features are usually needed for low-level work with many boards, where "low level" implies that the board initialization software may not be working. (That's a common reason to need JTAG tools. Another is to enable working with microcontroller-based systems, which often have no debugging support except a JTAG connector.)

Target config files may also export utility functions to board and user config files. Such functions should use name prefixes, to help avoid naming collisions.

Board files could also accept input variables from user config files. For example, there might be a `J4_JUMPER` setting used to identify what kind of flash memory a development board is using, or how to set up other clocks and peripherals.

6.2.2 Variable Naming Convention

Most boards have only one instance of a chip. However, it should be easy to create a board with more than one such chip (as shown above). Accordingly, we encourage these conventions for naming variables associated with different `target.cfg` files, to promote consistency and so that board files can override target defaults.

Inputs to target config files include:

- `CHIPNAME` ... This gives a name to the overall chip, and is used as part of tap identifier dotted names. While the default is normally provided by the chip manufacturer, board files may need to distinguish between instances of a chip.

- `ENDIAN` ... By default `little` - although chips may hard-wire `big`. Chips that can't change endianness don't need to use this variable.

- `CPUTAPID` ... When OpenOCD examines the JTAG chain, it can be told verify the chips against the JTAG IDCODE register. The target file will hold one or more defaults, but sometimes the chip in a board will use a different ID (perhaps a newer revision).

Outputs from target config files include:

- `_TARGETNAME` ... By convention, this variable is created by the target configuration script. The board configuration file may make use of this variable to configure things like a "reset init" script, or other things specific to that board and that target. If the chip has 2 targets, the names are `_TARGETNAME0`, `_TARGETNAME1`, ... etc.

6.2.3 The reset-init Event Handler

Board config files run in the OpenOCD configuration stage; they can't use TAPs or targets, since they haven't been fully set up yet. This means you can't write memory or access chip registers; you can't even verify that a flash chip is present. That's done later in event handlers, of which the target `reset-init` handler is one of the most important.

Except on microcontrollers, the basic job of `reset-init` event handlers is setting up flash and DRAM, as normally handled by boot loaders. Microcontrollers rarely use boot loaders; they run right out of their on-chip flash and SRAM memory. But they may want to use one of these handlers too, if just for developer convenience.

> **Note:** Because this is so very board-specific, and chip-specific, no examples are included here. Instead, look at the board config files distributed with OpenOCD. If you have a boot loader, its source code will help; so will configuration files for other JTAG tools (see [Translating Configuration Files], page 30).

Some of this code could probably be shared between different boards. For example, setting up a DRAM controller often doesn't differ by much except the bus width (16 bits or 32?) and memory timings, so a reusable TCL procedure loaded by the `target.cfg` file might take those as parameters. Similarly with oscillator, PLL, and clock setup; and disabling the watchdog. Structure the code cleanly, and provide comments to help the next developer doing such work. (*You might be that next person* trying to reuse init code!)

The last thing normally done in a `reset-init` handler is probing whatever flash memory was configured. For most chips that needs to be done while the associated target is halted, either because JTAG memory access uses the CPU or to prevent conflicting CPU access.

6.2.4 JTAG Clock Rate

Before your `reset-init` handler has set up the PLLs and clocking, you may need to run with a low JTAG clock rate. See [JTAG Speed], page 48. Then you'd increase that rate after your handler has made it possible to use the faster JTAG clock. When the initial low speed is board-specific, for example because it depends on a board-specific oscillator speed, then you should probably set it up in the board config file; if it's target-specific, it belongs in the target config file.

For most ARM-based processors the fastest JTAG clock[1] is one sixth of the CPU clock; or one eighth for ARM11 cores. Consult chip documentation to determine the peak JTAG clock rate, which might be less than that.

> **Warning:** On most ARMs, JTAG clock detection is coupled to the core clock, so software using a `wait for interrupt` operation blocks JTAG access. Adaptive clocking provides a partial workaround, but a more complete solution just avoids using that instruction with JTAG debuggers.

If both the chip and the board support adaptive clocking, use the `jtag_rclk` command, in case your board is used with JTAG adapter which also supports it. Otherwise use `adapter_khz`. Set the slow rate at the beginning of the reset sequence, and the faster rate as soon as the clocks are at full speed.

6.2.5 The init_board procedure

The concept of `init_board` procedure is very similar to `init_targets` (See [The init_targets procedure], page 29.) - it's a replacement of "linear" configuration scripts. This procedure is meant to be executed when OpenOCD enters run stage (See [Entering the Run Stage], page 32,) after `init_targets`. The idea to have separate `init_targets` and `init_board` procedures is to allow the first one to configure everything target specific (internal flash, internal RAM, etc.) and the second one to configure everything board specific (reset signals, chip frequency, reset-init event handler, external memory, etc.). Additionally "linear" board config file will most likely fail when target config file uses `init_targets` scheme ("linear" script is executed before `init` and `init_targets` - after), so separating these two configuration stages is very convenient, as the easiest way to overcome this problem is to convert board config file to use `init_board` procedure. Board config scripts don't need to override `init_targets` defined in target config files when they only need to add some specifics.

Just as `init_targets`, the `init_board` procedure can be overridden by "next level" script (which sources the original), allowing greater code reuse.

```
### board_file.cfg ###

# source target file that does most of the config in init_targets
```

---

[1] A FAQ http://www.arm.com/support/faqdev/4170.html gives details.

```
source [find target/target.cfg]

proc enable_fast_clock {} {
    # enables fast on-board clock source
    # configures the chip to use it
}

# initialize only board specifics - reset, clock, adapter frequency
proc init_board {} {
    reset_config trst_and_srst trst_pulls_srst

    $_TARGETNAME configure -event reset-init {
        adapter_khz 1
        enable_fast_clock
        adapter_khz 10000
    }
}
```

6.3 Target Config Files

Board config files communicate with target config files using naming conventions as described above, and may source one or more target config files like this:

```
source [find target/FOOBAR.cfg]
```

The point of a target config file is to package everything about a given chip that board config files need to know. In summary the target files should contain

1. Set defaults
2. Add TAPs to the scan chain
3. Add CPU targets (includes GDB support)
4. CPU/Chip/CPU-Core specific features
5. On-Chip flash

As a rule of thumb, a target file sets up only one chip. For a microcontroller, that will often include a single TAP, which is a CPU needing a GDB target, and its on-chip flash.

More complex chips may include multiple TAPs, and the target config file may need to define them all before OpenOCD can talk to the chip. For example, some phone chips have JTAG scan chains that include an ARM core for operating system use, a DSP, another ARM core embedded in an image processing engine, and other processing engines.

6.3.1 Default Value Boiler Plate Code

All target configuration files should start with code like this, letting board config files express environment-specific differences in how things should be set up.

```
# Boards may override chip names, perhaps based on role,
# but the default should match what the vendor uses
if { [info exists CHIPNAME] } {
    set  _CHIPNAME $CHIPNAME
} else {
```

```
      set  _CHIPNAME sam7x256
}

# ONLY use ENDIAN with targets that can change it.
if { [info exists ENDIAN] } {
   set  _ENDIAN $ENDIAN
} else {
   set  _ENDIAN little
}

# TAP identifiers may change as chips mature, for example with
# new revision fields (the "3" here). Pick a good default; you
# can pass several such identifiers to the "jtag newtap" command.
if { [info exists CPUTAPID ] } {
   set _CPUTAPID $CPUTAPID
} else {
   set _CPUTAPID 0x3f0f0f0f
}
```

Remember: Board config files may include multiple target config files, or the same target file multiple times (changing at least CHIPNAME).

Likewise, the target configuration file should define _TARGETNAME (or _TARGETNAME0 etc) and use it later on when defining debug targets:

```
set _TARGETNAME $_CHIPNAME.cpu
target create $_TARGETNAME arm7tdmi -chain-position $_TARGETNAME
```

6.3.2 Adding TAPs to the Scan Chain

After the "defaults" are set up, add the TAPs on each chip to the JTAG scan chain. See Chapter 10 [TAP Declaration], page 55, and the naming convention for taps.

In the simplest case the chip has only one TAP, probably for a CPU or FPGA. The config file for the Atmel AT91SAM7X256 looks (in part) like this:

```
jtag newtap $_CHIPNAME cpu -irlen 4 -expected-id $_CPUTAPID
```

A board with two such at91sam7 chips would be able to source such a config file twice, with different values for CHIPNAME, so it adds a different TAP each time.

If there are nonzero -expected-id values, OpenOCD attempts to verify the actual tap id against those values. It will issue error messages if there is mismatch, which can help to pinpoint problems in OpenOCD configurations.

```
JTAG tap: sam7x256.cpu tap/device found: 0x3f0f0f0f
            (Manufacturer: 0x787, Part: 0xf0f0, Version: 0x3)
ERROR: Tap: sam7x256.cpu - Expected id: 0x12345678, Got: 0x3f0f0f0f
ERROR: expected: mfg: 0x33c, part: 0x2345, ver: 0x1
ERROR:      got: mfg: 0x787, part: 0xf0f0, ver: 0x3
```

There are more complex examples too, with chips that have multiple TAPs. Ones worth looking at include:

• target/omap3530.cfg – with disabled ARM and DSP, plus a JRC to enable them

- `target/str912.cfg` – with flash, CPU, and boundary scan
- `target/ti_dm355.cfg` – with ETM, ARM, and JRC (this JRC is not currently used)

6.3.3 Add CPU targets

After adding a TAP for a CPU, you should set it up so that GDB and other commands can use it. See Chapter 11 [CPU Configuration], page 61. For the at91sam7 example above, the command can look like this; note that `$_ENDIAN` is not needed, since OpenOCD defaults to little endian, and this chip doesn't support changing that.

```
set _TARGETNAME $_CHIPNAME.cpu
target create $_TARGETNAME arm7tdmi -chain-position $_TARGETNAME
```

Work areas are small RAM areas associated with CPU targets. They are used by OpenOCD to speed up downloads, and to download small snippets of code to program flash chips. If the chip includes a form of "on-chip-ram" - and many do - define a work area if you can. Again using the at91sam7 as an example, this can look like:

```
$_TARGETNAME configure -work-area-phys 0x00200000 \
               -work-area-size 0x4000 -work-area-backup 0
```

6.3.4 Define CPU targets working in SMP

After setting targets, you can define a list of targets working in SMP.

```
set _TARGETNAME_1 $_CHIPNAME.cpu1
set _TARGETNAME_2 $_CHIPNAME.cpu2
target create $_TARGETNAME_1 cortex_a -chain-position $_CHIPNAME.dap \
-coreid 0 -dbgbase $_DAP_DBG1
target create $_TARGETNAME_2 cortex_a -chain-position $_CHIPNAME.dap \
-coreid 1 -dbgbase $_DAP_DBG2
#define 2 targets working in smp.
target smp $_CHIPNAME.cpu2 $_CHIPNAME.cpu1
```

In the above example on cortex_a, 2 cpus are working in SMP. In SMP only one GDB instance is created and :

- a set of hardware breakpoint sets the same breakpoint on all targets in the list.
- halt command triggers the halt of all targets in the list.
- resume command triggers the write context and the restart of all targets in the list.
- following a breakpoint: the target stopped by the breakpoint is displayed to the GDB session.
- dedicated GDB serial protocol packets are implemented for switching/retrieving the target displayed by the GDB session see [Using OpenOCD SMP with GDB], page 127.

The SMP behaviour can be disabled/enabled dynamically. On cortex_a following command have been implemented.

- cortex_a smp_on : enable SMP mode, behaviour is as described above.
- cortex_a smp_off : disable SMP mode, the current target is the one displayed in the GDB session, only this target is now controlled by GDB session. This behaviour is useful during system boot up.

- cortex_a smp_gdb : display/fix the core id displayed in GDB session see following example.

```
>cortex_a smp_gdb
gdb coreid  0 -> -1
#0 : coreid 0 is displayed to GDB ,
#-> -1 : next resume triggers a real resume
> cortex_a smp_gdb 1
gdb coreid  0 -> 1
#0 :coreid 0 is displayed to GDB ,
#->1  : next resume displays coreid 1 to GDB
> resume
> cortex_a smp_gdb
gdb coreid  1 -> 1
#1 :coreid 1 is displayed to GDB ,
#->1 : next resume displays coreid 1 to GDB
> cortex_a smp_gdb -1
gdb coreid  1 -> -1
#1 :coreid 1 is displayed to GDB,
#->-1 : next resume triggers a real resume
```

6.3.5 Chip Reset Setup

As a rule, you should put the **reset_config** command into the board file. Most things you think you know about a chip can be tweaked by the board.

Some chips have specific ways the TRST and SRST signals are managed. In the unusual case that these are *chip specific* and can never be changed by board wiring, they could go here. For example, some chips can't support JTAG debugging without both signals.

Provide a **reset-assert** event handler if you can. Such a handler uses JTAG operations to reset the target, letting this target config be used in systems which don't provide the optional SRST signal, or on systems where you don't want to reset all targets at once. Such a handler might write to chip registers to force a reset, use a JRC to do that (preferable – the target may be wedged!), or force a watchdog timer to trigger. (For Cortex-M targets, this is not necessary. The target driver knows how to use trigger an NVIC reset when SRST is not available.)

Some chips need special attention during reset handling if they're going to be used with JTAG. An example might be needing to send some commands right after the target's TAP has been reset, providing a **reset-deassert-post** event handler that writes a chip register to report that JTAG debugging is being done. Another would be reconfiguring the watchdog so that it stops counting while the core is halted in the debugger.

JTAG clocking constraints often change during reset, and in some cases target config files (rather than board config files) are the right places to handle some of those issues. For example, immediately after reset most chips run using a slower clock than they will use later. That means that after reset (and potentially, as OpenOCD first starts up) they must use a slower JTAG clock rate than they will use later. See [JTAG Speed], page 48.

> **Important:** When you are debugging code that runs right after chip reset, getting these issues right is critical. In particular, if you see intermittent failures

when OpenOCD verifies the scan chain after reset, look at how you are setting up JTAG clocking.

6.3.6 The init_targets procedure

Target config files can either be "linear" (script executed line-by-line when parsed in configuration stage, See [Configuration Stage], page 32,) or they can contain a special procedure called **init_targets**, which will be executed when entering run stage (after parsing all config files or after **init** command, See [Entering the Run Stage], page 32.) Such procedure can be overriden by "next level" script (which sources the original). This concept faciliates code reuse when basic target config files provide generic configuration procedures and **init_targets** procedure, which can then be sourced and enchanced or changed in a "more specific" target config file. This is not possible with "linear" config scripts, because sourcing them executes every initialization commands they provide.

```
### generic_file.cfg ###

proc setup_my_chip {chip_name flash_size ram_size} {
    # basic initialization procedure ...
}

proc init_targets {} {
    # initializes generic chip with 4kB of flash and 1kB of RAM
    setup_my_chip MY_GENERIC_CHIP 4096 1024
}

### specific_file.cfg ###

source [find target/generic_file.cfg]

proc init_targets {} {
    # initializes specific chip with 128kB of flash and 64kB of RAM
    setup_my_chip MY_CHIP_WITH_128K_FLASH_64KB_RAM 131072 65536
}
```

The easiest way to convert "linear" config files to **init_targets** version is to enclose every line of "code" (i.e. not **source** commands, procedures, etc.) in this procedure.

For an example of this scheme see LPC2000 target config files.

The **init_boards** procedure is a similar concept concerning board config files (See [The init_board procedure], page 24.)

6.3.7 The init_target_events procedure

A special procedure called **init_target_events** is run just after **init_targets** (See [The init_targets procedure], page 29.) and before **init_board** (See [The init_board procedure], page 24.) It is used to set up default target events for the targets that do not have those events already assigned.

6.3.8 ARM Core Specific Hacks

If the chip has a DCC, enable it. If the chip is an ARM9 with some special high speed download features - enable it.

If present, the MMU, the MPU and the CACHE should be disabled.

Some ARM cores are equipped with trace support, which permits examination of the instruction and data bus activity. Trace activity is controlled through an "Embedded Trace Module" (ETM) on one of the core's scan chains. The ETM emits voluminous data through a "trace port". (See [ARM Hardware Tracing], page 103.) If you are using an external trace port, configure it in your board config file. If you are using an on-chip "Embedded Trace Buffer" (ETB), configure it in your target config file.

```
etm config $_TARGETNAME 16 normal full etb
etb config $_TARGETNAME $_CHIPNAME.etb
```

6.3.9 Internal Flash Configuration

This applies **ONLY TO MICROCONTROLLERS** that have flash built in.

Never ever in the "target configuration file" define any type of flash that is external to the chip. (For example a BOOT flash on Chip Select 0.) Such flash information goes in a board file - not the TARGET (chip) file.

Examples:

- at91sam7x256 - has 256K flash YES enable it.
- str912 - has flash internal YES enable it.
- imx27 - uses boot flash on CS0 - it goes in the board file.
- pxa270 - again - CS0 flash - it goes in the board file.

6.4 Translating Configuration Files

If you have a configuration file for another hardware debugger or toolset (Abatron, BDI2000, BDI3000, CCS, Lauterbach, Segger, Macraigor, etc.), translating it into OpenOCD syntax is often quite straightforward. The most tricky part of creating a configuration script is oftentimes the reset init sequence where e.g. PLLs, DRAM and the like is set up.

One trick that you can use when translating is to write small Tcl procedures to translate the syntax into OpenOCD syntax. This can avoid manual translation errors and make it easier to convert other scripts later on.

Example of transforming quirky arguments to a simple search and replace job:

```
#     Lauterbach syntax(?)
#
#         Data.Set c15:0x042f %long 0x40000015
#
#     OpenOCD syntax when using procedure below.
#
#         setc15 0x01 0x00050078

proc setc15 {regs value} {
    global TARGETNAME
```

```
echo [format "set p15 0x%04x, 0x%08x" $regs $value]

arm mcr 15 [expr ($regs>>12)&0x7] \
    [expr ($regs>>0)&0xf] [expr ($regs>>4)&0xf] \
    [expr ($regs>>8)&0x7] $value
}
```

7 Daemon Configuration

The commands here are commonly found in the openocd.cfg file and are used to specify what TCP/IP ports are used, and how GDB should be supported.

7.1 Configuration Stage

When the OpenOCD server process starts up, it enters a *configuration stage* which is the only time that certain commands, *configuration commands*, may be issued. Normally, configuration commands are only available inside startup scripts.

In this manual, the definition of a configuration command is presented as a *Config Command*, not as a *Command* which may be issued interactively. The runtime `help` command also highlights configuration commands, and those which may be issued at any time.

Those configuration commands include declaration of TAPs, flash banks, the interface used for JTAG communication, and other basic setup. The server must leave the configuration stage before it may access or activate TAPs. After it leaves this stage, configuration commands may no longer be issued.

7.2 Entering the Run Stage

The first thing OpenOCD does after leaving the configuration stage is to verify that it can talk to the scan chain (list of TAPs) which has been configured. It will warn if it doesn't find TAPs it expects to find, or finds TAPs that aren't supposed to be there. You should see no errors at this point. If you see errors, resolve them by correcting the commands you used to configure the server. Common errors include using an initial JTAG speed that's too fast, and not providing the right IDCODE values for the TAPs on the scan chain.

Once OpenOCD has entered the run stage, a number of commands become available. A number of these relate to the debug targets you may have declared. For example, the `mww` command will not be available until a target has been successfuly instantiated. If you want to use those commands, you may need to force entry to the run stage.

`init`   [Config Command]
> This command terminates the configuration stage and enters the run stage. This helps when you need to have the startup scripts manage tasks such as resetting the target, programming flash, etc. To reset the CPU upon startup, add "init" and "reset" at the end of the config script or at the end of the OpenOCD command line using the `-c` command line switch.
>
> If this command does not appear in any startup/configuration file OpenOCD executes the command for you after processing all configuration files and/or command line options.
>
> **NOTE:** This command normally occurs at or near the end of your openocd.cfg file to force OpenOCD to "initialize" and make the targets ready. For example: If your openocd.cfg file needs to read/write memory on your target, `init` must occur before the memory read/write commands. This includes **nand probe**.

`jtag_init`   [Overridable Procedure]
> This is invoked at server startup to verify that it can talk to the scan chain (list of TAPs) which has been configured.

The default implementation first tries `jtag arp_init`, which uses only a lightweight JTAG reset before examining the scan chain. If that fails, it tries again, using a harder reset from the overridable procedure `init_reset`.

Implementations must have verified the JTAG scan chain before they return. This is done by calling `jtag arp_init` (or `jtag arp_init-reset`).

7.3 TCP/IP Ports

The OpenOCD server accepts remote commands in several syntaxes. Each syntax uses a different TCP/IP port, which you may specify only during configuration (before those ports are opened).

For reasons including security, you may wish to prevent remote access using one or more of these ports. In such cases, just specify the relevant port number as zero. If you disable all access through TCP/IP, you will need to use the command line `-pipe` option.

`gdb_port` [*number*]   [Command]

> Normally gdb listens to a TCP/IP port, but GDB can also communicate via pipes(stdin/out or named pipes). The name "gdb_port" stuck because it covers probably more than 90% of the normal use cases.
>
> No arguments reports GDB port. "pipe" means listen to stdin output to stdout, an integer is base port number, "disable" disables the gdb server.
>
> When using "pipe", also use log_output to redirect the log output to a file so as not to flood the stdin/out pipes.
>
> The -p/-pipe option is deprecated and a warning is printed as it is equivalent to passing in -c "gdb_port pipe; log_output openocd.log".
>
> Any other string is interpreted as named pipe to listen to. Output pipe is the same name as input pipe, but with 'o' appended, e.g. /var/gdb, /var/gdbo.
>
> The GDB port for the first target will be the base port, the second target will listen on gdb_port + 1, and so on. When not specified during the configuration stage, the port *number* defaults to 3333.

`tcl_port` [*number*]   [Command]

> Specify or query the port used for a simplified RPC connection that can be used by clients to issue TCL commands and get the output from the Tcl engine. Intended as a machine interface. When not specified during the configuration stage, the port *number* defaults to 6666.

`telnet_port` [*number*]   [Command]

> Specify or query the port on which to listen for incoming telnet connections. This port is intended for interaction with one human through TCL commands. When not specified during the configuration stage, the port *number* defaults to 4444. When specified as zero, this port is not activated.

7.4 GDB Configuration

You can reconfigure some GDB behaviors if needed. The ones listed here are static and global. See [Target Configuration], page 63, about configuring individual targets. See [Target Events], page 66, about configuring target-specific event handling.

`gdb_breakpoint_override [hard|soft|disable]`   [Command]
>   Force breakpoint type for gdb **break** commands. This option supports GDB GUIs
>   which don't distinguish hard versus soft breakpoints, if the default OpenOCD and
>   GDB behaviour is not sufficient. GDB normally uses hardware breakpoints if the
>   memory map has been set up for flash regions.

`gdb_flash_program (enable|disable)`   [Config Command]
>   Set to **enable** to cause OpenOCD to program the flash memory when a vFlash packet
>   is received. The default behaviour is **enable**.

`gdb_memory_map (enable|disable)`   [Config Command]
>   Set to **enable** to cause OpenOCD to send the memory configuration to GDB when
>   requested. GDB will then know when to set hardware breakpoints, and program flash
>   using the GDB load command. **gdb_flash_program enable** must also be enabled for
>   flash programming to work. Default behaviour is **enable**. See [gdb_flash_program],
>   page 34.

`gdb_report_data_abort (enable|disable)`   [Config Command]
>   Specifies whether data aborts cause an error to be reported by GDB memory read
>   packets. The default behaviour is **disable**; use **enable** see these errors reported.

`gdb_target_description (enable|disable)`   [Config Command]
>   Set to **enable** to cause OpenOCD to send the target descriptions to gdb via
>   qXfer:features:read packet. The default behaviour is **enable**.

`gdb_save_tdesc`   [Command]
>   Saves the target descripton file to the local file system.
>
>   The file name is *target_name*.xml.

7.5 Event Polling

Hardware debuggers are parts of asynchronous systems, where significant events can happen
at any time. The OpenOCD server needs to detect some of these events, so it can report
them to through TCL command line or to GDB.

Examples of such events include:

- One of the targets can stop running ... maybe it triggers a code breakpoint or data
  watchpoint, or halts itself.
- Messages may be sent over "debug message" channels ... many targets support such
  messages sent over JTAG, for receipt by the person debugging or tools.
- Loss of power ... some adapters can detect these events.
- Resets not issued through JTAG ... such reset sources can include button presses
  or other system hardware, sometimes including the target itself (perhaps through a
  watchdog).
- Debug instrumentation sometimes supports event triggering such as "trace buffer full"
  (so it can quickly be emptied) or other signals (to correlate with code behavior).

None of those events are signaled through standard JTAG signals. However, most conventions for JTAG connectors include voltage level and system reset (SRST) signal detection.

Some connectors also include instrumentation signals, which can imply events when those signals are inputs.

In general, OpenOCD needs to periodically check for those events, either by looking at the status of signals on the JTAG connector or by sending synchronous "tell me your status" JTAG requests to the various active targets. There is a command to manage and monitor that polling, which is normally done in the background.

poll [on|off]   [Command]
    Poll the current target for its current state. (Also, see [target curstate], page 66.) If that target is in debug mode, architecture specific information about the current state is printed. An optional parameter allows background polling to be enabled and disabled.

    You could use this from the TCL command shell, or from GDB using `monitor poll` command. Leave background polling enabled while you're using GDB.

```
> poll
background polling: on
target state: halted
target halted in ARM state due to debug-request, \
                current mode: Supervisor
cpsr: 0x800000d3 pc: 0x11081bfc
MMU: disabled, D-Cache: disabled, I-Cache: enabled
>
```

8 Debug Adapter Configuration

Correctly installing OpenOCD includes making your operating system give OpenOCD access to debug adapters. Once that has been done, Tcl commands are used to select which one is used, and to configure how it is used.

> **Note:** Because OpenOCD started out with a focus purely on JTAG, you may find places where it wrongly presumes JTAG is the only transport protocol in use. Be aware that recent versions of OpenOCD are removing that limitation. JTAG remains more functional than most other transports. Other transports do not support boundary scan operations, or may be specific to a given chip vendor. Some might be usable only for programming flash memory, instead of also for debugging.

Debug Adapters/Interfaces/Dongles are normally configured through commands in an interface configuration file which is sourced by your `openocd.cfg` file, or through a command line `-f interface/....cfg` option.

```
source [find interface/olimex-jtag-tiny.cfg]
```

These commands tell OpenOCD what type of JTAG adapter you have, and how to talk to it. A few cases are so simple that you only need to say what driver to use:

```
# jlink interface
interface jlink
```

Most adapters need a bit more configuration than that.

8.1 Interface Configuration

The interface command tells OpenOCD what type of debug adapter you are using. Depending on the type of adapter, you may need to use one or more additional commands to further identify or configure the adapter.

interface *name*   [Config Command]
> Use the interface driver *name* to connect to the target.

interface_list   [Command]
> List the debug adapter drivers that have been built into the running copy of OpenOCD.

interface transports *transport_name+*   [Command]
> Specifies the transports supported by this debug adapter. The adapter driver builds-in similar knowledge; use this only when external configuration (such as jumpering) changes what the hardware can support.

adapter_name   [Command]
> Returns the name of the debug adapter driver being used.

8.2 Interface Drivers

Each of the interface drivers listed here must be explicitly enabled when OpenOCD is configured, in order to be made available at run time.

amt_jtagaccel   [Interface Driver]

> Amontec Chameleon in its JTAG Accelerator configuration, connected to a PC's EPP mode parallel port. This defines some driver-specific commands:

> **parport_port** *number*   [Config Command]
>> Specifies either the address of the I/O port (default: 0x378 for LPT1) or the number of the **/dev/parport** device.

> **rtck** [**enable**|**disable**]   [Config Command]
>> Displays status of RTCK option. Optionally sets that option first.

arm-jtag-ew   [Interface Driver]

> Olimex ARM-JTAG-EW USB adapter This has one driver-specific command:

> **armjtagew_info**   [Command]
>> Logs some status

at91rm9200   [Interface Driver]

> Supports bitbanged JTAG from the local system, presuming that system is an Atmel AT91rm9200 and a specific set of GPIOs is used.

cmsis-dap   [Interface Driver]

> ARM CMSIS-DAP compliant based adapter.

> **cmsis_dap_vid_pid** [*vid pid*]+   [Config Command]
>> The vendor ID and product ID of the CMSIS-DAP device. If not specified the driver will attempt to auto detect the CMSIS-DAP device. Currently, up to eight [*vid, pid*] pairs may be given, e.g.

>> **cmsis_dap_vid_pid 0xc251 0xf001 0x0d28 0x0204**

> **cmsis_dap_serial** [*serial*]   [Config Command]
>> Specifies the *serial* of the CMSIS-DAP device to use. If not specified, serial numbers are not considered.

> **cmsis-dap info**   [Command]
>> Display various device information, like hardware version, firmware version, current bus status.

dummy   [Interface Driver]

> A dummy software-only driver for debugging.

ep93xx   [Interface Driver]

> Cirrus Logic EP93xx based single-board computer bit-banging (in development)

ft2232   [Interface Driver]
     FTDI FT2232 (USB) based devices over one of the userspace libraries.

     Note that this driver has several flaws and the `ftdi` driver is recommended as its replacement.

     These interfaces have several commands, used to configure the driver before initializing the JTAG scan chain:

`ft2232_device_desc` *description*   [Config Command]
     Provides the USB device description (the *iProduct string*) of the FTDI FT2232 device. If not specified, the FTDI default value is used. This setting is only valid if compiled with FTD2XX support.

`ft2232_serial` *serial-number*   [Config Command]
     Specifies the *serial-number* of the FTDI FT2232 device to use, in case the vendor provides unique IDs and more than one FT2232 device is connected to the host. If not specified, serial numbers are not considered. (Note that USB serial numbers can be arbitrary Unicode strings, and are not restricted to containing only decimal digits.)

`ft2232_layout` *name*   [Config Command]
     Each vendor's FT2232 device can use different GPIO signals to control output-enables, reset signals, and LEDs. Currently valid layout *name* values include:

- **axm0432_jtag** Axiom AXM-0432
- **comstick** Hitex STR9 comstick
- **cortino** Hitex Cortino JTAG interface
- **evb_lm3s811** TI/Luminary Micro EVB_LM3S811 as a JTAG interface, either for the local Cortex-M3 (SRST only) or in a passthrough mode (neither SRST nor TRST) This layout can not support the SWO trace mechanism, and should be used only for older boards (before rev C).
- **luminary_icdi** This layout should be used with most TI/Luminary eval boards, including Rev C LM3S811 eval boards and the eponymous ICDI boards, to debug either the local Cortex-M3 or in passthrough mode to debug some other target. It can support the SWO trace mechanism.
- **flyswatter** Tin Can Tools Flyswatter
- **icebear** ICEbear JTAG adapter from Section 5
- **jtagkey** Amontec JTAGkey and JTAGkey-Tiny (and compatibles)
- **jtagkey2** Amontec JTAGkey2 (and compatibles)
- **m5960** American Microsystems M5960
- **olimex-jtag** Olimex ARM-USB-OCD and ARM-USB-Tiny
- **oocdlink** OOCDLink
- **redbee-econotag** Integrated with a Redbee development board.
- **redbee-usb** Integrated with a Redbee USB-stick development board.
- **sheevaplug** Marvell Sheevaplug development kit
- **signalyzer** Xverve Signalyzer

> — **stm32stick** Hitex STM32 Performance Stick
>
> — **turtelizer2** egnite Software turtelizer2
>
> — **usbjtag** "USBJTAG-1" layout described in the OpenOCD diploma thesis

ft2232_vid_pid [*vid pid*]+   [Config Command]
> The vendor ID and product ID of the FTDI FT2232 device. If not specified, the FTDI default values are used. Currently, up to eight [*vid*, *pid*] pairs may be given, e.g.
>
>   ft2232_vid_pid 0x0403 0xcff8 0x15ba 0x0003

ft2232_latency *ms*   [Config Command]
> On some systems using FT2232 based JTAG interfaces the FT_Read function call in ft2232_read() fails to return the expected number of bytes. This can be caused by USB communication delays and has proved hard to reproduce and debug. Setting the FT2232 latency timer to a larger value increases delays for short USB packets but it also reduces the risk of timeouts before receiving the expected number of bytes. The OpenOCD default value is 2 and for some systems a value of 10 has proved useful.

ft2232_channel *channel*   [Config Command]
> Used to select the channel of the ft2232 chip to use (between 1 and 4). The default value is 1.

For example, the interface config file for a Turtelizer JTAG Adapter looks something like this:

    interface ft2232
    ft2232_device_desc "Turtelizer JTAG/RS232 Adapter"
    ft2232_layout turtelizer2
    ft2232_vid_pid 0x0403 0xbdc8

ftdi   [Interface Driver]
This driver is for adapters using the MPSSE (Multi-Protocol Synchronous Serial Engine) mode built into many FTDI chips, such as the FT2232, FT4232 and FT232H. It is a complete rewrite to address a large number of problems with the ft2232 interface driver.

The driver is using libusb-1.0 in asynchronous mode to talk to the FTDI device, bypassing intermediate libraries like libftdi of D2XX. Performance-wise it is consistently faster than the ft2232 driver, sometimes several times faster.

A major improvement of this driver is that support for new FTDI based adapters can be added competely through configuration files, without the need to patch and rebuild OpenOCD.

The driver uses a signal abstraction to enable Tcl configuration files to define outputs for one or several FTDI GPIO. These outputs can then be controlled using the **ftdi_set_signal** command. Special signal names are reserved for nTRST, nSRST and LED (for blink) so that they, if defined, will be used for their customary purpose.

Depending on the type of buffer attached to the FTDI GPIO, the outputs have to be controlled differently. In order to support tristateable signals such as nSRST, both a data GPIO and an output-enable GPIO can be specified for each signal. The following output buffer configurations are supported:

— Push-pull with one FTDI output as (non-)inverted data line
— Open drain with one FTDI output as (non-)inverted output-enable
— Tristate with one FTDI output as (non-)inverted data line and another FTDI output as (non-)inverted output-enable
— Unbuffered, using the FTDI GPIO as a tristate output directly by switching data and direction as necessary

These interfaces have several commands, used to configure the driver before initializing the JTAG scan chain:

ftdi_vid_pid [*vid pid*]+   [Config Command]
> The vendor ID and product ID of the adapter. If not specified, the FTDI default values are used. Currently, up to eight [*vid*, *pid*] pairs may be given, e.g.
>
> ```
> ftdi_vid_pid 0x0403 0xcff8 0x15ba 0x0003
> ```

ftdi_device_desc *description*   [Config Command]
> Provides the USB device description (the *iProduct string*) of the adapter. If not specified, the device description is ignored during device selection.

ftdi_serial *serial-number*   [Config Command]
> Specifies the *serial-number* of the adapter to use, in case the vendor provides unique IDs and more than one adapter is connected to the host. If not specified, serial numbers are not considered. (Note that USB serial numbers can be arbitrary Unicode strings, and are not restricted to containing only decimal digits.)

ftdi_channel *channel*   [Config Command]
> Selects the channel of the FTDI device to use for MPSSE operations. Most adapters use the default, channel 0, but there are exceptions.

ftdi_layout_init *data direction*   [Config Command]
> Specifies the initial values of the FTDI GPIO data and direction registers. Each value is a 16-bit number corresponding to the concatenation of the high and low FTDI GPIO registers. The values should be selected based on the schematics of the adapter, such that all signals are set to safe levels with minimal impact on the target system. Avoid floating inputs, conflicting outputs and initially asserted reset signals.

ftdi_layout_signal *name* [**-data**|**-ndata** *data_mask*]   [Config Command]
> [**-oe**|**-noe** *oe_mask*] [**-alias**|**-nalias** *name*]
> Creates a signal with the specified *name*, controlled by one or more FTDI GPIO pins via a range of possible buffer connections. The masks are FTDI GPIO register bitmasks to tell the driver the connection and type of the output buffer driving the respective signal. *data_mask* is the bitmask for the pin(s) connected to the data input of the output buffer. **-ndata** is used with inverting data inputs and **-data** with non-inverting inputs. The **-oe** (or **-noe**) option

tells where the output-enable (or not-output-enable) input to the output buffer is connected.

Both *data_mask* and *oe_mask* need not be specified. For example, a simple open-collector transistor driver would be specified with `-oe` only. In that case the signal can only be set to drive low or to Hi-Z and the driver will complain if the signal is set to drive high. Which means that if it's a reset signal, `reset_config` must be specified as `srst_open_drain`, not `srst_push_pull`.

A special case is provided when `-data` and `-oe` is set to the same bitmask. Then the FTDI pin is considered being connected straight to the target without any buffer. The FTDI pin is then switched between output and input as necessary to provide the full set of low, high and Hi-Z characteristics. In all other cases, the pins specified in a signal definition are always driven by the FTDI.

If `-alias` or `-nalias` is used, the signal is created identical (or with data inverted) to an already specified signal *name*.

`ftdi_set_signal` *name* `0|1|z`   [Command]
> Set a previously defined signal to the specified level.
>
> — `0`, drive low
>
> — `1`, drive high
>
> — `z`, set to high-impedance

For example adapter definitions, see the configuration files shipped in the `interface/ftdi` directory.

`remote_bitbang`   [Interface Driver]
> Drive JTAG from a remote process. This sets up a UNIX or TCP socket connection with a remote process and sends ASCII encoded bitbang requests to that process instead of directly driving JTAG.
>
> The remote_bitbang driver is useful for debugging software running on processors which are being simulated.

`remote_bitbang_port` *number*   [Config Command]
> Specifies the TCP port of the remote process to connect to or 0 to use UNIX sockets instead of TCP.

`remote_bitbang_host` *hostname*   [Config Command]
> Specifies the hostname of the remote process to connect to using TCP, or the name of the UNIX socket to use if remote_bitbang_port is 0.

For example, to connect remotely via TCP to the host foobar you might have something like:

```
interface remote_bitbang
remote_bitbang_port 3335
remote_bitbang_host foobar
```

To connect to another process running locally via UNIX sockets with socket named mysocket:

```
interface remote_bitbang
remote_bitbang_port 0
remote_bitbang_host mysocket
```

usb_blaster [Interface Driver]

USB JTAG/USB-Blaster compatibles over one of the userspace libraries for FTDI chips. These interfaces have several commands, used to configure the driver before initializing the JTAG scan chain:

usb_blaster_device_desc *description* [Config Command]

Provides the USB device description (the *iProduct string*) of the FTDI FT245 device. If not specified, the FTDI default value is used. This setting is only valid if compiled with FTD2XX support.

usb_blaster_vid_pid *vid pid* [Config Command]

The vendor ID and product ID of the FTDI FT245 device. If not specified, default values are used. Currently, only one *vid*, *pid* pair may be given, e.g. for Altera USB-Blaster (default):

```
usb_blaster_vid_pid 0x09FB 0x6001
```

The following VID/PID is for Kolja Waschk's USB JTAG:

```
usb_blaster_vid_pid 0x16C0 0x06AD
```

usb_blaster_pin (pin6|pin8) (0|1|s|t) [Command]

Sets the state or function of the unused GPIO pins on USB-Blasters (pins 6 and 8 on the female JTAG header). These pins can be used as SRST and/or TRST provided the appropriate connections are made on the target board.

For example, to use pin 6 as SRST:

```
usb_blaster_pin pin6 s
reset_config srst_only
```

usb_blaster_lowlevel_driver (ftdi|ftd2xx|ublast2) [Command]

Chooses the low level access method for the adapter. If not specified, `ftdi` is selected unless it wasn't enabled during the configure stage. USB-Blaster II needs `ublast2`.

usb_blaster_firmware *path* [Command]

This command specifies *path* to access USB-Blaster II firmware image. To be used with USB-Blaster II only.

gw16012 [Interface Driver]

Gateworks GW16012 JTAG programmer. This has one driver-specific command:

parport_port [*port_number*] [Config Command]

Display either the address of the I/O port (default: 0x378 for LPT1) or the number of the **/dev/parport** device. If a parameter is provided, first switch to use that port. This is a write-once setting.

`jlink`   [Interface Driver]
> Segger J-Link family of USB adapters. It currently supports JTAG and SWD transports.
>
> > **Compatibility Note:** Segger released many firmware versions for the many harware versions they produced. OpenOCD was extensively tested and intended to run on all of them, but some combinations were reported as incompatible. As a general recommendation, it is advisable to use the latest firmware version available for each hardware version. However the current V8 is a moving target, and Segger firmware versions released after the OpenOCD was released may not be compatible. In such cases it is recommended to revert to the last known functional version. For 0.5.0, this is from "Feb 8 2012 14:30:39", packed with 4.42c. For 0.6.0, the last known version is from "May 3 2012 18:36:22", packed with 4.46f.

> `jlink caps`   [Command]
> > Display the device firmware capabilities.

> `jlink info`   [Command]
> > Display various device information, like hardware version, firmware version, current bus status.

> `jlink hw_jtag [2|3]`   [Command]
> > Set the JTAG protocol version to be used. Without argument, show the actual JTAG protocol version.

> `jlink config`   [Command]
> > Display the J-Link configuration.

> `jlink config kickstart [`*val*`]`   [Command]
> > Set the Kickstart power on JTAG-pin 19. Without argument, show the Kickstart configuration.

> `jlink config mac_address [ff:ff:ff:ff:ff:ff]`   [Command]
> > Set the MAC address of the J-Link Pro. Without argument, show the MAC address.

> `jlink config ip [A.B.C.D(/E|F.G.H.I)]`   [Command]
> > Set the IP configuration of the J-Link Pro, where A.B.C.D is the IP address, E the bit of the subnet mask and F.G.H.I the subnet mask. Without arguments, show the IP configuration.

> `jlink config usb_address [0x00 `*to*` 0x03 `*or*` 0xff]`   [Command]
> > Set the USB address; this will also change the product id. Without argument, show the USB address.

> `jlink config reset`   [Command]
> > Reset the current configuration.

> `jlink config save`   [Command]
> > Save the current configuration to the internal persistent storage.

`jlink pid` *val*   [Config]

> Set the USB PID of the interface. As a configuration command, it can be used only before 'init'.

`jlink serial` *serial-number*   [Config]

> Set the *serial-number* of the interface, in case more than one adapter is connected to the host. If not specified, serial numbers are not considered.
>
> Note that there may be leading zeros in the *serial-number* string that will not show in the Segger software, but must be specified here. Debug level 3 output contains serial numbers if there is a mismatch.
>
> As a configuration command, it can be used only before 'init'.

`parport`   [Interface Driver]

> Supports PC parallel port bit-banging cables: Wigglers, PLD download cable, and more. These interfaces have several commands, used to configure the driver before initializing the JTAG scan chain:

`parport_cable` *name*   [Config Command]

> Set the layout of the parallel port cable used to connect to the target. This is a write-once setting. Currently valid cable *name* values include:
>
> — **altium** Altium Universal JTAG cable.
> — **arm-jtag** Same as original wiggler except SRST and TRST connections reversed and TRST is also inverted.
> — **chameleon** The Amontec Chameleon's CPLD when operated in configuration mode. This is only used to program the Chameleon itself, not a connected target.
> — **dlc5** The Xilinx Parallel cable III.
> — **flashlink** The ST Parallel cable.
> — **lattice** Lattice ispDOWNLOAD Cable
> — **old_amt_wiggler** The Wiggler configuration that comes with some versions of Amontec's Chameleon Programmer. The new version available from the website uses the original Wiggler layout ('*wiggler*')
> — **triton** The parallel port adapter found on the "Karo Triton 1 Development Board". This is also the layout used by the HollyGates design (see `http://www.lartmaker.nl/projects/jtag/`).
> — **wiggler** The original Wiggler layout, also supported by several clones, such as the Olimex ARM-JTAG
> — **wiggler2** Same as original wiggler except an led is fitted on D5.
> — **wiggler_ntrst_inverted** Same as original wiggler except TRST is inverted.

`parport_port` [*port_number*]   [Config Command]

> Display either the address of the I/O port (default: 0x378 for LPT1) or the number of the `/dev/parport` device. If a parameter is provided, first switch to use that port. This is a write-once setting.
>
> When using PPDEV to access the parallel port, use the number of the parallel port: `parport_port 0` (the default). If `parport_port 0x378` is specified you may encounter a problem.

`parport_toggling_time` [*nanoseconds*]   [Command]
> Displays how many nanoseconds the hardware needs to toggle TCK; the parport driver uses this value to obey the `adapter_khz` configuration. When the optional *nanoseconds* parameter is given, that setting is changed before displaying the current value.
>
> The default setting should work reasonably well on commodity PC hardware. However, you may want to calibrate for your specific hardware.
>
> > **Tip:** To measure the toggling time with a logic analyzer or a digital storage oscilloscope, follow the procedure below:
> >
> > ```
> > > parport_toggling_time 1000
> > > adapter_khz 500
> > ```
> >
> > This sets the maximum JTAG clock speed of the hardware, but the actual speed probably deviates from the requested 500 kHz. Now, measure the time between the two closest spaced TCK transitions. You can use `runtest 1000` or something similar to generate a large set of samples. Update the setting to match your measurement:
> >
> > ```
> > > parport_toggling_time <measured nanoseconds>
> > ```
> >
> > Now the clock speed will be a better match for `adapter_khz rate` commands given in OpenOCD scripts and event handlers.
> >
> > You can do something similar with many digital multimeters, but note that you'll probably need to run the clock continuously for several seconds before it decides what clock rate to show. Adjust the toggling time up or down until the measured clock rate is a good match for the adapter_khz rate you specified; be conservative.

`parport_write_on_exit` (on|off)   [Config Command]
> This will configure the parallel driver to write a known cable-specific value to the parallel interface on exiting OpenOCD.

For example, the interface configuration file for a classic "Wiggler" cable on LPT2 might look something like this:

```
interface parport
parport_port 0x278
parport_cable wiggler
```

`presto`   [Interface Driver]
> ASIX PRESTO USB JTAG programmer.

`presto_serial` *serial_string*   [Config Command]
> Configures the USB serial number of the Presto device to use.

`rlink`   [Interface Driver]
> Raisonance RLink USB adapter

`usbprog`   [Interface Driver]
> usbprog is a freely programmable USB adapter.

vsllink   [Interface Driver]
> vsllink is part of Versaloon which is a versatile USB programmer.
>> **Note:** This defines quite a few driver-specific commands, which are not currently documented here.

hla   [Interface Driver]
> This is a driver that supports multiple High Level Adapters. This type of adapter does not expose some of the lower level api's that OpenOCD would normally use to access the target.
>
> Currently supported adapters include the ST STLINK and TI ICDI. STLINK firmware version >= V2.J21.S4 recommended due to issues with earlier versions of firmware where serial number is reset after first use. Suggest using ST firmware update utility to upgrade STLINK firmware even if current version reported is V2.J21.S4.

> **hla_device_desc** *description*   [Config Command]
>> Currently Not Supported.

> **hla_serial** *serial*   [Config Command]
>> Specifies the serial number of the adapter.

> **hla_layout (stlink|icdi)**   [Config Command]
>> Specifies the adapter layout to use.

> **hla_vid_pid** *vid pid*   [Config Command]
>> The vendor ID and product ID of the device.

> **hla_command** *command*   [Command]
>> Execute a custom adapter-specific command. The *command* string is passed as is to the underlying adapter layout handler.

opendous   [Interface Driver]
> opendous-jtag is a freely programmable USB adapter.

ulink   [Interface Driver]
> This is the Keil ULINK v1 JTAG debugger.

ZY1000   [Interface Driver]
> This is the Zylin ZY1000 JTAG debugger.
>
> **Note:** This defines some driver-specific commands, which are not currently documented here.

power [on|off]   [Command]
> Turn power switch to target on/off. No arguments: print status.

bcm2835gpio   [Interface Driver]
> This SoC is present in Raspberry Pi which is a cheap single-board computer exposing some GPIOs on its expansion header.
>
> The driver accesses memory-mapped GPIO peripheral registers directly for maximum performance, but the only possible race condition is for the pins' modes/muxing

(which is highly unlikely), so it should be able to coexist nicely with both sysfs bitbanging and various peripherals' kernel drivers. The driver restores the previous configuration on exit.

See `interface/raspberrypi-native.cfg` for a sample config and pinout.

8.3 Transport Configuration

As noted earlier, depending on the version of OpenOCD you use, and the debug adapter you are using, several transports may be available to communicate with debug targets (or perhaps to program flash memory).

`transport list`   [Command]
>   displays the names of the transports supported by this version of OpenOCD.

`transport select transport_name`   [Command]
>   Select which of the supported transports to use in this OpenOCD session.
>
>   When invoked with `transport_name`, attempts to select the named transport. The transport must be supported by the debug adapter hardware and by the version of OpenOCD you are using (including the adapter's driver).
>
>   If no transport has been selected and no `transport_name` is provided, `transport select` auto-selects the first transport supported by the debug adapter.
>
>   `transport select` always returns the name of the session's selected transport, if any.

8.3.1 JTAG Transport

JTAG is the original transport supported by OpenOCD, and most of the OpenOCD commands support it. JTAG transports expose a chain of one or more Test Access Points (TAPs), each of which must be explicitly declared. JTAG supports both debugging and boundary scan testing. Flash programming support is built on top of debug support.

JTAG transport is selected with the command `transport select jtag`. Unless your adapter uses [hla_interface], page 46, in which case the command is `transport select hla_jtag`.

8.3.2 SWD Transport

SWD (Serial Wire Debug) is an ARM-specific transport which exposes one Debug Access Point (DAP, which must be explicitly declared. (SWD uses fewer signal wires than JTAG.) SWD is debug-oriented, and does not support boundary scan testing. Flash programming support is built on top of debug support. (Some processors support both JTAG and SWD.)

SWD transport is selected with the command `transport select swd`. Unless your adapter uses [hla_interface], page 46, in which case the command is `transport select hla_swd`.

`swd newdap ...`   [Command]
>   Declares a single DAP which uses SWD transport. Parameters are currently the same as "jtag newtap" but this is expected to change.

`swd wcr trn prescale`   [Command]
>   Updates TRN (turnaround delay) and prescaling.fields of the Wire Control Register (WCR). No parameters: displays current settings.

8.3.3 SPI Transport

The Serial Peripheral Interface (SPI) is a general purpose transport which uses four wire signaling. Some processors use it as part of a solution for flash programming.

8.4 JTAG Speed

JTAG clock setup is part of system setup. It *does not belong with interface setup* since any interface only knows a few of the constraints for the JTAG clock speed. Sometimes the JTAG speed is changed during the target initialization process: (1) slow at reset, (2) program the CPU clocks, (3) run fast. Both the "slow" and "fast" clock rates are functions of the oscillators used, the chip, the board design, and sometimes power management software that may be active.

The speed used during reset, and the scan chain verification which follows reset, can be adjusted using a `reset-start` target event handler. It can then be reconfigured to a faster speed by a `reset-init` target event handler after it reprograms those CPU clocks, or manually (if something else, such as a boot loader, sets up those clocks). See [Target Events], page 66. When the initial low JTAG speed is a chip characteristic, perhaps because of a required oscillator speed, provide such a handler in the target config file. When that speed is a function of a board-specific characteristic such as which speed oscillator is used, it belongs in the board config file instead. In both cases it's safest to also set the initial JTAG clock rate to that same slow speed, so that OpenOCD never starts up using a clock speed that's faster than the scan chain can support.

```
jtag_rclk 3000
$_TARGET.cpu configure -event reset-start { jtag_rclk 3000 }
```

If your system supports adaptive clocking (RTCK), configuring JTAG to use that is probably the most robust approach. However, it introduces delays to synchronize clocks; so it may not be the fastest solution.

NOTE: Script writers should consider using `jtag_rclk` instead of `adapter_khz`, but only for (ARM) cores and boards which support adaptive clocking.

adapter_khz *max_speed_kHz*   [Command]
> A non-zero speed is in KHZ. Hence: 3000 is 3mhz. JTAG interfaces usually support a limited number of speeds. The speed actually used won't be faster than the speed specified.
>
> Chip data sheets generally include a top JTAG clock rate. The actual rate is often a function of a CPU core clock, and is normally less than that peak rate. For example, most ARM cores accept at most one sixth of the CPU clock.
>
> Speed 0 (khz) selects RTCK method. See [FAQ RTCK], page 133. If your system uses RTCK, you won't need to change the JTAG clocking after setup. Not all interfaces, boards, or targets support "rtck". If the interface device can not support it, an error is returned when you try to use RTCK.

jtag_rclk *fallback_speed_kHz*   [Function]
> This Tcl proc (defined in `startup.tcl`) attempts to enable RTCK/RCLK. If that fails (maybe the interface, board, or target doesn't support it), falls back to the specified frequency.

```
# Fall back to 3mhz if RTCK is not supported
jtag_rclk 3000
```

9 Reset Configuration

Every system configuration may require a different reset configuration. This can also be quite confusing. Resets also interact with *reset-init* event handlers, which do things like setting up clocks and DRAM, and JTAG clock rates. (See [JTAG Speed], page 48.) They can also interact with JTAG routers. Please see the various board files for examples.

> **Note:** To maintainers and integrators: Reset configuration touches several things at once. Normally the board configuration file should define it and assume that the JTAG adapter supports everything that's wired up to the board's JTAG connector.

> However, the target configuration file could also make note of something the silicon vendor has done inside the chip, which will be true for most (or all) boards using that chip. And when the JTAG adapter doesn't support everything, the user configuration file will need to override parts of the reset configuration provided by other files.

9.1 Types of Reset

There are many kinds of reset possible through JTAG, but they may not all work with a given board and adapter. That's part of why reset configuration can be error prone.

- *System Reset* ... the *SRST* hardware signal resets all chips connected to the JTAG adapter, such as processors, power management chips, and I/O controllers. Normally resets triggered with this signal behave exactly like pressing a RESET button.
- *JTAG TAP Reset* ... the *TRST* hardware signal resets just the TAP controllers connected to the JTAG adapter. Such resets should not be visible to the rest of the system; resetting a device's TAP controller just puts that controller into a known state.
- *Emulation Reset* ... many devices can be reset through JTAG commands. These resets are often distinguishable from system resets, either explicitly (a "reset reason" register says so) or implicitly (not all parts of the chip get reset).
- *Other Resets* ... system-on-chip devices often support several other types of reset. You may need to arrange that a watchdog timer stops while debugging, preventing a watchdog reset. There may be individual module resets.

In the best case, OpenOCD can hold SRST, then reset the TAPs via TRST and send commands through JTAG to halt the CPU at the reset vector before the 1st instruction is executed. Then when it finally releases the SRST signal, the system is halted under debugger control before any code has executed. This is the behavior required to support the **reset halt** and **reset init** commands; after **reset init** a board-specific script might do things like setting up DRAM. (See [Reset Command], page 98.)

9.2 SRST and TRST Issues

Because SRST and TRST are hardware signals, they can have a variety of system-specific constraints. Some of the most common issues are:

- *Signal not available* ... Some boards don't wire SRST or TRST to the JTAG connector. Some JTAG adapters don't support such signals even if they are wired up. Use the **reset_config** *signals* options to say when either of those signals is not connected.

When SRST is not available, your code might not be able to rely on controllers having been fully reset during code startup. Missing TRST is not a problem, since JTAG-level resets can be triggered using with TMS signaling.

- *Signals shorted* ... Sometimes a chip, board, or adapter will connect SRST to TRST, instead of keeping them separate. Use the `reset_config` *combination* options to say when those signals aren't properly independent.

- *Timing* ... Reset circuitry like a resistor/capacitor delay circuit, reset supervisor, or on-chip features can extend the effect of a JTAG adapter's reset for some time after the adapter stops issuing the reset. For example, there may be chip or board requirements that all reset pulses last for at least a certain amount of time; and reset buttons commonly have hardware debouncing. Use the `adapter_nsrst_delay` and `jtag_ntrst_delay` commands to say when extra delays are needed.

- *Drive type* ... Reset lines often have a pullup resistor, letting the JTAG interface treat them as open-drain signals. But that's not a requirement, so the adapter may need to use push/pull output drivers. Also, with weak pullups it may be advisable to drive signals to both levels (push/pull) to minimize rise times. Use the `reset_config` *trst_type* and *srst_type* parameters to say how to drive reset signals.

- *Special initialization* ... Targets sometimes need special JTAG initialization sequences to handle chip-specific issues (not limited to errata). For example, certain JTAG commands might need to be issued while the system as a whole is in a reset state (SRST active) but the JTAG scan chain is usable (TRST inactive). Many systems treat combined assertion of SRST and TRST as a trigger for a harder reset than SRST alone. Such custom reset handling is discussed later in this chapter.

There can also be other issues. Some devices don't fully conform to the JTAG specifications. Trivial system-specific differences are common, such as SRST and TRST using slightly different names. There are also vendors who distribute key JTAG documentation for their chips only to developers who have signed a Non-Disclosure Agreement (NDA).

Sometimes there are chip-specific extensions like a requirement to use the normally-optional TRST signal (precluding use of JTAG adapters which don't pass TRST through), or needing extra steps to complete a TAP reset.

In short, SRST and especially TRST handling may be very finicky, needing to cope with both architecture and board specific constraints.

9.3 Commands for Handling Resets

`adapter_nsrst_assert_width` *milliseconds*   [Command]
>   Minimum amount of time (in milliseconds) OpenOCD should wait after asserting nSRST (active-low system reset) before allowing it to be deasserted.

`adapter_nsrst_delay` *milliseconds*   [Command]
>   How long (in milliseconds) OpenOCD should wait after deasserting nSRST (active-low system reset) before starting new JTAG operations. When a board has a reset button connected to SRST line it will probably have hardware debouncing, implying you should use this.

`jtag_ntrst_assert_width` *milliseconds*   [Command]
> Minimum amount of time (in milliseconds) OpenOCD should wait after asserting nTRST (active-low JTAG TAP reset) before allowing it to be deasserted.

`jtag_ntrst_delay` *milliseconds*   [Command]
> How long (in milliseconds) OpenOCD should wait after deasserting nTRST (active-low JTAG TAP reset) before starting new JTAG operations.

`reset_config` *mode_flag ...*   [Command]
> This command displays or modifies the reset configuration of your combination of JTAG board and target in target configuration scripts.
>
> Information earlier in this section describes the kind of problems the command is intended to address (see [SRST and TRST Issues], page 50). As a rule this command belongs only in board config files, describing issues like *board doesn't connect TRST*; or in user config files, addressing limitations derived from a particular combination of interface and board. (An unlikely example would be using a TRST-only adapter with a board that only wires up SRST.)
>
> The *mode_flag* options can be specified in any order, but only one of each type – *signals*, *combination*, *gates*, *trst_type*, *srst_type* and *connect_type* – may be specified at a time. If you don't provide a new value for a given type, its previous value (perhaps the default) is unchanged. For example, this means that you don't need to say anything at all about TRST just to declare that if the JTAG adapter should want to drive SRST, it must explicitly be driven high (`srst_push_pull`).
>
> - *signals* can specify which of the reset signals are connected. For example, If the JTAG interface provides SRST, but the board doesn't connect that signal properly, then OpenOCD can't use it. Possible values are `none` (the default), `trst_only`, `srst_only` and `trst_and_srst`.
>
>   > **Tip:** If your board provides SRST and/or TRST through the JTAG connector, you must declare that so those signals can be used.
>
> - The *combination* is an optional value specifying broken reset signal implementations. The default behaviour if no option given is `separate`, indicating everything behaves normally. `srst_pulls_trst` states that the test logic is reset together with the reset of the system (e.g. NXP LPC2000, "broken" board layout), `trst_pulls_srst` says that the system is reset together with the test logic (only hypothetical, I haven't seen hardware with such a bug, and can be worked around). `combined` implies both `srst_pulls_trst` and `trst_pulls_srst`.
>
> - The *gates* tokens control flags that describe some cases where JTAG may be unvailable during reset. `srst_gates_jtag` (default) indicates that asserting SRST gates the JTAG clock. This means that no communication can happen on JTAG while SRST is asserted. Its converse is `srst_nogate`, indicating that JTAG commands can safely be issued while SRST is active.
>
> - The *connect_type* tokens control flags that describe some cases where SRST is asserted while connecting to the target. `srst_nogate` is required to use this option. `connect_deassert_srst` (default) indicates that SRST will not be asserted while connecting to the target. Its converse is `connect_assert_srst`, indicating that SRST will be asserted before any target connection. Only some targets

support this feature, STM32 and STR9 are examples. This feature is useful if you are unable to connect to your target due to incorrect options byte config or illegal program execution.

The optional *trst_type* and *srst_type* parameters allow the driver mode of each reset line to be specified. These values only affect JTAG interfaces with support for different driver modes, like the Amontec JTAGkey and JTAG Accelerator. Also, they are necessarily ignored if the relevant signal (TRST or SRST) is not connected.

- Possible *trst_type* driver modes for the test reset signal (TRST) are the default `trst_push_pull`, and `trst_open_drain`. Most boards connect this signal to a pulldown, so the JTAG TAPs never leave reset unless they are hooked up to a JTAG adapter.

- Possible *srst_type* driver modes for the system reset signal (SRST) are the default `srst_open_drain`, and `srst_push_pull`. Most boards connect this signal to a pullup, and allow the signal to be pulled low by various events including system powerup and pressing a reset button.

9.4 Custom Reset Handling

OpenOCD has several ways to help support the various reset mechanisms provided by chip and board vendors. The commands shown in the previous section give standard parameters. There are also *event handlers* associated with TAPs or Targets. Those handlers are Tcl procedures you can provide, which are invoked at particular points in the reset sequence.

When SRST is not an option you must set up a `reset-assert` event handler for your target. For example, some JTAG adapters don't include the SRST signal; and some boards have multiple targets, and you won't always want to reset everything at once.

After configuring those mechanisms, you might still find your board doesn't start up or reset correctly. For example, maybe it needs a slightly different sequence of SRST and/or TRST manipulations, because of quirks that the `reset_config` mechanism doesn't address; or asserting both might trigger a stronger reset, which needs special attention.

Experiment with lower level operations, such as `jtag_reset` and the `jtag arp_*` operations shown here, to find a sequence of operations that works. See Chapter 17 [JTAG Commands], page 119. When you find a working sequence, it can be used to override `jtag_init`, which fires during OpenOCD startup (see [Configuration Stage], page 32); or `init_reset`, which fires during reset processing.

You might also want to provide some project-specific reset schemes. For example, on a multi-target board the standard `reset` command would reset all targets, but you may need the ability to reset only one target at time and thus want to avoid using the board-wide SRST signal.

`init_reset` *mode*   [Overridable Procedure]
> This is invoked near the beginning of the `reset` command, usually to provide as much of a cold (power-up) reset as practical. By default it is also invoked from `jtag_init` if the scan chain does not respond to pure JTAG operations. The *mode* parameter is the parameter given to the low level reset command (`halt`, `init`, or `run`), `setup`, or potentially some other value.

The default implementation just invokes `jtag arp_init-reset`. Replacements will normally build on low level JTAG operations such as `jtag_reset`. Operations here must not address individual TAPs (or their associated targets) until the JTAG scan chain has first been verified to work.

Implementations must have verified the JTAG scan chain before they return. This is done by calling `jtag arp_init` (or `jtag arp_init-reset`).

`jtag arp_init`   [Command]

This validates the scan chain using just the four standard JTAG signals (TMS, TCK, TDI, TDO). It starts by issuing a JTAG-only reset. Then it performs checks to verify that the scan chain configuration matches the TAPs it can observe. Those checks include checking IDCODE values for each active TAP, and verifying the length of their instruction registers using TAP `-ircapture` and `-irmask` values. If these tests all pass, TAP `setup` events are issued to all TAPs with handlers for that event.

`jtag arp_init-reset`   [Command]

This uses TRST and SRST to try resetting everything on the JTAG scan chain (and anything else connected to SRST). It then invokes the logic of `jtag arp_init`.

10 TAP Declaration

Test Access Ports (TAPs) are the core of JTAG. TAPs serve many roles, including:

- **Debug Target** A CPU TAP can be used as a GDB debug target.
- **Flash Programming** Some chips program the flash directly via JTAG. Others do it indirectly, making a CPU do it.
- **Program Download** Using the same CPU support GDB uses, you can initialize a DRAM controller, download code to DRAM, and then start running that code.
- **Boundary Scan** Most chips support boundary scan, which helps test for board assembly problems like solder bridges and missing connections.

OpenOCD must know about the active TAPs on your board(s). Setting up the TAPs is the core task of your configuration files. Once those TAPs are set up, you can pass their names to code which sets up CPUs and exports them as GDB targets, probes flash memory, performs low-level JTAG operations, and more.

10.1 Scan Chains

TAPs are part of a hardware *scan chain*, which is a daisy chain of TAPs. They also need to be added to OpenOCD's software mirror of that hardware list, giving each member a name and associating other data with it. Simple scan chains, with a single TAP, are common in systems with a single microcontroller or microprocessor. More complex chips may have several TAPs internally. Very complex scan chains might have a dozen or more TAPs: several in one chip, more in the next, and connecting to other boards with their own chips and TAPs.

You can display the list with the `scan_chain` command. (Don't confuse this with the list displayed by the `targets` command, presented in the next chapter. That only displays TAPs for CPUs which are configured as debugging targets.) Here's what the scan chain might look like for a chip more than one TAP:

```
   TapName               Enabled IdCode     Expected    IrLen IrCap IrMask
-- ------------------- ------- ---------- ---------- ----- ----- ------
 0 omap5912.dsp             Y   0x03df1d81 0x03df1d81    38 0x01  0x03
 1 omap5912.arm             Y   0x0692602f 0x0692602f     4 0x01  0x0f
 2 omap5912.unknown         Y   0x00000000 0x00000000     8 0x01  0x03
```

OpenOCD can detect some of that information, but not all of it. See [Autoprobing], page 59. Unfortunately, those TAPs can't always be autoconfigured, because not all devices provide good support for that. JTAG doesn't require supporting IDCODE instructions, and chips with JTAG routers may not link TAPs into the chain until they are told to do so.

The configuration mechanism currently supported by OpenOCD requires explicit configuration of all TAP devices using `jtag newtap` commands, as detailed later in this chapter. A command like this would declare one tap and name it `chip1.cpu`:

```
    jtag newtap chip1 cpu -irlen 4 -expected-id 0x3ba00477
```

Each target configuration file lists the TAPs provided by a given chip. Board configuration files combine all the targets on a board, and so forth. Note that *the order in which TAPs are declared is very important*. That declaration order must match the order in the JTAG scan chain, both inside a single chip and between them. See [FAQ TAP Order], page 136.

For example, the ST Microsystems STR912 chip has three separate TAPs[1]. To configure those taps, `target/str912.cfg` includes commands something like this:

```
jtag newtap str912 flash ... params ...
jtag newtap str912 cpu ... params ...
jtag newtap str912 bs ... params ...
```

Actual config files typically use a variable such as `$_CHIPNAME` instead of literals like `str912`, to support more than one chip of each type. See Chapter 6 [Config File Guidelines], page 21.

`jtag names`   [Command]

> Returns the names of all current TAPs in the scan chain. Use `jtag cget` or `jtag tapisenabled` to examine attributes and state of each TAP.
>
> ```
> foreach t [jtag names] {
>     puts [format "TAP: %s\n" $t]
> }
> ```

`scan_chain`   [Command]

> Displays the TAPs in the scan chain configuration, and their status. The set of TAPs listed by this command is fixed by exiting the OpenOCD configuration stage, but systems with a JTAG router can enable or disable TAPs dynamically.

10.2 TAP Names

When TAP objects are declared with `jtag newtap`, a *dotted.name* is created for the TAP, combining the name of a module (usually a chip) and a label for the TAP. For example: `xilinx.tap`, `str912.flash`, `omap3530.jrc`, `dm6446.dsp`, or `stm32.cpu`. Many other commands use that dotted.name to manipulate or refer to the TAP. For example, CPU configuration uses the name, as does declaration of NAND or NOR flash banks.

The components of a dotted name should follow "C" symbol name rules: start with an alphabetic character, then numbers and underscores are OK; while others (including dots!) are not.

10.3 TAP Declaration Commands

`jtag newtap` *chipname tapname configparams...*   [Command]

> Declares a new TAP with the dotted name *chipname.tapname*, and configured according to the various *configparams*.
>
> The *chipname* is a symbolic name for the chip. Conventionally target config files use `$_CHIPNAME`, defaulting to the model name given by the chip vendor but overridable.
>
> The *tapname* reflects the role of that TAP, and should follow this convention:
>
> - `bs` – For boundary scan if this is a separate TAP;
> - `cpu` – The main CPU of the chip, alternatively `arm` and `dsp` on chips with both ARM and DSP CPUs, `arm1` and `arm2` on chips with two ARMs, and so forth;
> - `etb` – For an embedded trace buffer (example: an ARM ETB11);

---

[1] See the ST document titled: *STR91xFAxxx, Section 3.15 Jtag Interface, Page: 28/102, Figure 3: JTAG chaining inside the STR91xFA.* http://eu.st.com/stonline/products/literature/ds/13495.pdf

- `flash` – If the chip has a flash TAP, like the str912;
- `jrc` – For JTAG route controller (example: the ICEPick modules on many Texas Instruments chips, like the OMAP3530 on Beagleboards);
- `tap` – Should be used only for FPGA- or CPLD-like devices with a single TAP;
- `unknownN` – If you have no idea what the TAP is for (N is a number);
- *when in doubt* – Use the chip maker's name in their data sheet. For example, the Freescale i.MX31 has a SDMA (Smart DMA) with a JTAG TAP; that TAP should be named `sdma`.

Every TAP requires at least the following *configparams*:

- `-irlen` *NUMBER*
  The length in bits of the instruction register, such as 4 or 5 bits.

A TAP may also provide optional *configparams*:

- `-disable` (or `-enable`)
  Use the `-disable` parameter to flag a TAP which is not linked into the scan chain after a reset using either TRST or the JTAG state machine's RESET state. You may use `-enable` to highlight the default state (the TAP is linked in). See [Enabling and Disabling TAPs], page 58.

- `-expected-id` *NUMBER*
  A non-zero *number* represents a 32-bit IDCODE which you expect to find when the scan chain is examined. These codes are not required by all JTAG devices. *Repeat the option* as many times as required if more than one ID code could appear (for example, multiple versions). Specify *number* as zero to suppress warnings about IDCODE values that were found but not included in the list.

  Provide this value if at all possible, since it lets OpenOCD tell when the scan chain it sees isn't right. These values are provided in vendors' chip documentation, usually a technical reference manual. Sometimes you may need to probe the JTAG hardware to find these values. See [Autoprobing], page 59.

- `-ignore-version`
  Specify this to ignore the JTAG version field in the `-expected-id` option. When vendors put out multiple versions of a chip, or use the same JTAG-level ID for several largely-compatible chips, it may be more practical to ignore the version field than to update config files to handle all of the various chip IDs. The version field is defined as bit 28-31 of the IDCODE.

- `-ircapture` *NUMBER*
  The bit pattern loaded by the TAP into the JTAG shift register on entry to the IRCAPTURE state, such as 0x01. JTAG requires the two LSBs of this value to be 01. By default, `-ircapture` and `-irmask` are set up to verify that two-bit value. You may provide additional bits if you know them, or indicate that a TAP doesn't conform to the JTAG specification.

- `-irmask` *NUMBER*
  A mask used with `-ircapture` to verify that instruction scans work correctly. Such scans are not used by OpenOCD except to verify that there seems to be no problems with JTAG scan chain operations.

10.4 Other TAP commands

jtag cget *dotted.name* -event *event_name*   [Command]
jtag configure *dotted.name* -event *event_name handler*   [Command]

> At this writing this TAP attribute mechanism is used only for event handling. (It is not a direct analogue of the cget/configure mechanism for debugger targets.) See the next section for information about the available events.
>
> The configure subcommand assigns an event handler, a TCL string which is evaluated when the event is triggered. The cget subcommand returns that handler.

10.5 TAP Events

OpenOCD includes two event mechanisms. The one presented here applies to all JTAG TAPs. The other applies to debugger targets, which are associated with certain TAPs.

The TAP events currently defined are:

- **post-reset**
  The TAP has just completed a JTAG reset. The tap may still be in the JTAG RESET state. Handlers for these events might perform initialization sequences such as issuing TCK cycles, TMS sequences to ensure exit from the ARM SWD mode, and more.

  Because the scan chain has not yet been verified, handlers for these events *should not issue commands which scan the JTAG IR or DR registers* of any particular target. **NOTE:** As this is written (September 2009), nothing prevents such access.

- **setup**
  The scan chain has been reset and verified. This handler may enable TAPs as needed.

- **tap-disable**
  The TAP needs to be disabled. This handler should implement jtag tapdisable by issuing the relevant JTAG commands.

- **tap-enable**
  The TAP needs to be enabled. This handler should implement jtag tapenable by issuing the relevant JTAG commands.

If you need some action after each JTAG reset which isn't actually specific to any TAP (since you can't yet trust the scan chain's contents to be accurate), you might:

```
jtag configure CHIP.jrc -event post-reset {
  echo "JTAG Reset done"
  ... non-scan jtag operations to be done after reset
}
```

10.6 Enabling and Disabling TAPs

In some systems, a *JTAG Route Controller* (JRC) is used to enable and/or disable specific JTAG TAPs. Many ARM-based chips from Texas Instruments include an "ICEPick" module, which is a JRC. Such chips include DaVinci and OMAP3 processors.

A given TAP may not be visible until the JRC has been told to link it into the scan chain; and if the JRC has been told to unlink that TAP, it will no longer be visible. Such routers address problems that JTAG "bypass mode" ignores, such as:

- The scan chain can only go as fast as its slowest TAP.
- Having many TAPs slows instruction scans, since all TAPs receive new instructions.
- TAPs in the scan chain must be powered up, which wastes power and prevents debugging some power management mechanisms.

The IEEE 1149.1 JTAG standard has no concept of a "disabled" tap, as implied by the existence of JTAG routers. However, the upcoming IEEE 1149.7 framework (layered on top of JTAG) does include a kind of JTAG router functionality.

In OpenOCD, tap enabling/disabling is invoked by the Tcl commands shown below, and is implemented using TAP event handlers. So for example, when defining a TAP for a CPU connected to a JTAG router, your `target.cfg` file should define TAP event handlers using code that looks something like this:

```
jtag configure CHIP.cpu -event tap-enable {
    ... jtag operations using CHIP.jrc
}
jtag configure CHIP.cpu -event tap-disable {
    ... jtag operations using CHIP.jrc
}
```

Then you might want that CPU's TAP enabled almost all the time:

```
jtag configure $CHIP.jrc -event setup "jtag tapenable $CHIP.cpu"
```

Note how that particular setup event handler declaration uses quotes to evaluate $CHIP when the event is configured. Using brackets { } would cause it to be evaluated later, at runtime, when it might have a different value.

jtag tapdisable *dotted.name*   [Command]
> If necessary, disables the tap by sending it a `tap-disable` event. Returns the string "1" if the tap specified by *dotted.name* is enabled, and "0" if it is disabled.

jtag tapenable *dotted.name*   [Command]
> If necessary, enables the tap by sending it a `tap-enable` event. Returns the string "1" if the tap specified by *dotted.name* is enabled, and "0" if it is disabled.

jtag tapisenabled *dotted.name*   [Command]
> Returns the string "1" if the tap specified by *dotted.name* is enabled, and "0" if it is disabled.
>
> > **Note:** Humans will find the `scan_chain` command more helpful for querying the state of the JTAG taps.

10.7 Autoprobing

TAP configuration is the first thing that needs to be done after interface and reset configuration. Sometimes it's hard finding out what TAPs exist, or how they are identified. Vendor documentation is not always easy to find and use.

To help you get past such problems, OpenOCD has a limited *autoprobing* ability to look at the scan chain, doing a *blind interrogation* and then reporting the TAPs it finds. To use this mechanism, start the OpenOCD server with only data that configures your JTAG interface, and arranges to come up with a slow clock (many devices don't support fast JTAG clocks right when they come out of reset).

For example, your `openocd.cfg` file might have:

```
source [find interface/olimex-arm-usb-tiny-h.cfg]
reset_config trst_and_srst
jtag_rclk 8
```

When you start the server without any TAPs configured, it will attempt to autoconfigure the TAPs. There are two parts to this:

1. *TAP discovery* ... After a JTAG reset (sometimes a system reset may be needed too), each TAP's data registers will hold the contents of either the IDCODE or BYPASS register. If JTAG communication is working, OpenOCD will see each TAP, and report what -expected-id to use with it.

2. *IR Length discovery* ... Unfortunately JTAG does not provide a reliable way to find out the value of the -irlen parameter to use with a TAP that is discovered. If OpenOCD can discover the length of a TAP's instruction register, it will report it. Otherwise you may need to consult vendor documentation, such as chip data sheets or BSDL files.

In many cases your board will have a simple scan chain with just a single device. Here's what OpenOCD reported with one board that's a bit more complex:

```
clock speed 8 kHz
There are no enabled taps. AUTO PROBING MIGHT NOT WORK!!
AUTO auto0.tap - use "jtag newtap auto0 tap -expected-id 0x2b900f0f ..."
AUTO auto1.tap - use "jtag newtap auto1 tap -expected-id 0x07926001 ..."
AUTO auto2.tap - use "jtag newtap auto2 tap -expected-id 0x0b73b02f ..."
AUTO auto0.tap - use "... -irlen 4"
AUTO auto1.tap - use "... -irlen 4"
AUTO auto2.tap - use "... -irlen 6"
no gdb ports allocated as no target has been specified
```

Given that information, you should be able to either find some existing config files to use, or create your own. If you create your own, you would configure from the bottom up: first a `target.cfg` file with these TAPs, any targets associated with them, and any on-chip resources; then a `board.cfg` with off-chip resources, clocking, and so forth.

11 CPU Configuration

This chapter discusses how to set up GDB debug targets for CPUs. You can also access these targets without GDB (see Chapter 16 [Architecture and Core Commands], page 103, and [Target State handling], page 97) and through various kinds of NAND and NOR flash commands. If you have multiple CPUs you can have multiple such targets.

We'll start by looking at how to examine the targets you have, then look at how to add one more target and how to configure it.

11.1 Target List

All targets that have been set up are part of a list, where each member has a name. That name should normally be the same as the TAP name. You can display the list with the `targets` (plural!) command. This display often has only one CPU; here's what it might look like with more than one:

```
     TargetName         Type       Endian TapName            State
 --  ------------------ ---------- ------ ------------------ ------------
  0* at91rm9200.cpu     arm920t    little at91rm9200.cpu     running
  1  MyTarget           cortex_m   little mychip.foo         tap-disabled
```

One member of that list is the *current target*, which is implicitly referenced by many commands. It's the one marked with a * near the target name. In particular, memory addresses often refer to the address space seen by that current target. Commands like `mdw` (memory display words) and `flash erase_address` (erase NOR flash blocks) are examples; and there are many more.

Several commands let you examine the list of targets:

target current   [Command]
> Returns the name of the current target.

target names   [Command]
> Lists the names of all current targets in the list.
>
> ```
> foreach t [target names] {
>     puts [format "Target: %s\n" $t]
> }
> ```

targets [*name*]   [Command]
> *Note: the name of this command is plural. Other target command names are singular.*
>
> With no parameter, this command displays a table of all known targets in a user friendly form.
>
> With a parameter, this command sets the current target to the given target with the given *name*; this is only relevant on boards which have more than one target.

Chapter 11: CPU Configuration

11.2 Target CPU Types

Each target has a *CPU type*, as shown in the output of the `targets` command. You need to specify that type when calling `target create`. The CPU type indicates more than just the instruction set. It also indicates how that instruction set is implemented, what kind of debug support it integrates, whether it has an MMU (and if so, what kind), what core-specific commands may be available (see Chapter 16 [Architecture and Core Commands], page 103), and more.

It's easy to see what target types are supported, since there's a command to list them.

target types   [Command]
    Lists all supported target types. At this writing, the supported CPU types are:
- `arm11` – this is a generation of ARMv6 cores
- `arm720t` – this is an ARMv4 core with an MMU
- `arm7tdmi` – this is an ARMv4 core
- `arm920t` – this is an ARMv4 core with an MMU
- `arm926ejs` – this is an ARMv5 core with an MMU
- `arm966e` – this is an ARMv5 core
- `arm9tdmi` – this is an ARMv4 core
- `avr` – implements Atmel's 8-bit AVR instruction set. (Support for this is preliminary and incomplete.)
- `cortex_a` – this is an ARMv7 core with an MMU
- `cortex_m` – this is an ARMv7 core, supporting only the compact Thumb2 instruction set.
- `dragonite` – resembles arm966e
- `dsp563xx` – implements Freescale's 24-bit DSP. (Support for this is still incomplete.)
- `fa526` – resembles arm920 (w/o Thumb)
- `feroceon` – resembles arm926
- `mips_m4k` – a MIPS core
- `xscale` – this is actually an architecture, not a CPU type. It is based on the ARMv5 architecture.
- `openrisc` – this is an OpenRISC 1000 core. The current implementation supports three JTAG TAP cores:
  - `OpenCores TAP` (See: jtag)
  - `Altera Virtual JTAG TAP` (See: http://www.altera.com/literature/ug/ug_virtualjtag.pdf)
  - `Xilinx BSCAN_*` virtual JTAG interface (See: http://www.xilinx.com/support/documentation/sw_manuals/xilinx14_2/spartan6_hdl.pdf)

  And two debug interfaces cores:
  - `Advanced debug interface` (See: adv_debug_sys)
  - `SoC Debug Interface` (See: dbg_interface)

To avoid being confused by the variety of ARM based cores, remember this key point: *ARM is a technology licencing company.* (See: http://www.arm.com.) The CPU name used by OpenOCD will reflect the CPU design that was licenced, not a vendor brand which incorporates that design. Name prefixes like arm7, arm9, arm11, and cortex reflect design generations; while names like ARMv4, ARMv5, ARMv6, and ARMv7 reflect an architecture version implemented by a CPU design.

11.3 Target Configuration

Before creating a "target", you must have added its TAP to the scan chain. When you've added that TAP, you will have a **dotted.name** which is used to set up the CPU support. The chip-specific configuration file will normally configure its CPU(s) right after it adds all of the chip's TAPs to the scan chain.

Although you can set up a target in one step, it's often clearer if you use shorter commands and do it in two steps: create it, then configure optional parts. All operations on the target after it's created will use a new command, created as part of target creation.

The two main things to configure after target creation are a work area, which usually has target-specific defaults even if the board setup code overrides them later; and event handlers (see [Target Events], page 66), which tend to be much more board-specific. The key steps you use might look something like this

```
target create MyTarget cortex_m -chain-position mychip.cpu
$MyTarget configure -work-area-phys 0x08000 -work-area-size 8096
$MyTarget configure -event reset-deassert-pre { jtag_rclk 5 }
$MyTarget configure -event reset-init { myboard_reinit }
```

You should specify a working area if you can; typically it uses some on-chip SRAM. Such a working area can speed up many things, including bulk writes to target memory; flash operations like checking to see if memory needs to be erased; GDB memory checksumming; and more.

> **Warning:** On more complex chips, the work area can become inaccessible when application code (such as an operating system) enables or disables the MMU. For example, the particular MMU context used to acess the virtual address will probably matter ... and that context might not have easy access to other addresses needed. At this writing, OpenOCD doesn't have much MMU intelligence.

It's often very useful to define a **reset-init** event handler. For systems that are normally used with a boot loader, common tasks include updating clocks and initializing memory controllers. That may be needed to let you write the boot loader into flash, in order to "de-brick" your board; or to load programs into external DDR memory without having run the boot loader.

target create *target_name type configparams...*   [Command]
> This command creates a GDB debug target that refers to a specific JTAG tap. It enters that target into a list, and creates a new command (**target_name**) which is used for various purposes including additional configuration.
>
> • *target_name* ... is the name of the debug target. By convention this should be the same as the *dotted.name* of the TAP associated with this target, which must be specified here using the **-chain-position** *dotted.name* configparam.

This name is also used to create the target object command, referred to here as `$target_name`, and in other places the target needs to be identified.

- *type* ... specifies the target type. See [target types], page 62.

- *configparams* ... all parameters accepted by `$target_name configure` are permitted. If the target is big-endian, set it here with `-endian big`.

    You *must* set the `-chain-position` *dotted.name* here.

`$target_name configure` *configparams...*   [Command]

The options accepted by this command may also be specified as parameters to `target create`. Their values can later be queried one at a time by using the `$target_name cget` command.

Warning: changing some of these after setup is dangerous. For example, moving a target from one TAP to another; and changing its endianness.

- `-chain-position` *dotted.name* – names the TAP used to access this target.

- `-endian (big|little)` – specifies whether the CPU uses big or little endian conventions

- `-event` *event_name event_body* – See [Target Events], page 66. Note that this updates a list of named event handlers. Calling this twice with two different event names assigns two different handlers, but calling it twice with the same event name assigns only one handler.

- `-work-area-backup (0|1)` – says whether the work area gets backed up; by default, *it is not backed up.* When possible, use a working_area that doesn't need to be backed up, since performing a backup slows down operations. For example, the beginning of an SRAM block is likely to be used by most build systems, but the end is often unused.

- `-work-area-size` *size* – specify work are size, in bytes. The same size applies regardless of whether its physical or virtual address is being used.

- `-work-area-phys` *address* – set the work area base *address* to be used when no MMU is active.

- `-work-area-virt` *address* – set the work area base *address* to be used when an MMU is active. *Do not specify a value for this except on targets with an MMU.* The value should normally correspond to a static mapping for the `-work-area-phys` address, set up by the current operating system.

- `-rtos` *rtos_type* – enable rtos support for target, *rtos_type* can be one of `auto|eCos|ThreadX| FreeRTOS|linux|ChibiOS|embKernel|mqx` See [RTOS Support], page 128.

11.4 Other $target_name Commands

The Tcl/Tk language has the concept of object commands, and OpenOCD adopts that same model for targets.

A good Tk example is a on screen button. Once a button is created a button has a name (a path in Tk terms) and that name is useable as a first class command. For example in Tk, one can create a button and later configure it like this:

```
# Create
button .foobar -background red -command { foo }
# Modify
.foobar configure -foreground blue
# Query
set x [.foobar cget -background]
# Report
puts [format "The button is %s" $x]
```

In OpenOCD's terms, the "target" is an object just like a Tcl/Tk button, and its object commands are invoked the same way.

```
str912.cpu    mww 0x1234 0x42
omap3530.cpu  mww 0x5555 123
```

The commands supported by OpenOCD target objects are:

$target_name arp_examine   [Command]
$target_name arp_halt   [Command]
$target_name arp_poll   [Command]
$target_name arp_reset   [Command]
$target_name arp_waitstate   [Command]

> Internal OpenOCD scripts (most notably `startup.tcl`) use these to deal with specific reset cases. They are not otherwise documented here.

$target_name array2mem *arrayname width address count*   [Command]
$target_name mem2array *arrayname width address count*   [Command]

> These provide an efficient script-oriented interface to memory. The `array2mem` primitive writes bytes, halfwords, or words; while `mem2array` reads them. In both cases, the TCL side uses an array, and the target side uses raw memory.
>
> The efficiency comes from enabling the use of bulk JTAG data transfer operations. The script orientation comes from working with data values that are packaged for use by TCL scripts; `mdw` type primitives only print data they retrieve, and neither store nor return those values.
>
> - *arrayname* ... is the name of an array variable
> - *width* ... is 8/16/32 - indicating the memory access size
> - *address* ... is the target memory address
> - *count* ... is the number of elements to process

$target_name cget *queryparm*   [Command]

> Each configuration parameter accepted by **$target_name configure** can be individually queried, to return its current value. The *queryparm* is a parameter name accepted by that command, such as **-work-area-phys**. There are a few special cases:
>
> - **-event** *event_name* – returns the handler for the event named *event_name*. This is a special case because setting a handler requires two parameters.
> - **-type** – returns the target type. This is a special case because this is set using **target create** and can't be changed using **$target_name configure**.
>
> For example, if you wanted to summarize information about all the targets you might use something like this:

```
foreach name [target names] {
    set y [$name cget -endian]
    set z [$name cget -type]
    puts [format "Chip %d is %s, Endian: %s, type: %s" \
                  $x $name $y $z]
}
```

$target_name curstate   [Command]

> Displays the current target state: debug-running, halted, reset, running, or unknown. (Also, see [Event Polling], page 34.)

$target_name eventlist   [Command]

> Displays a table listing all event handlers currently associated with this target. See [Target Events], page 66.

$target_name invoke-event *event_name*   [Command]

> Invokes the handler for the event named *event_name*. (This is primarily intended for use by OpenOCD framework code, for example by the reset code in startup.tcl.)

$target_name mdw *addr* [*count*]   [Command]
$target_name mdh *addr* [*count*]   [Command]
$target_name mdb *addr* [*count*]   [Command]

> Display contents of address *addr*, as 32-bit words (mdw), 16-bit halfwords (mdh), or 8-bit bytes (mdb). If *count* is specified, displays that many units. (If you want to manipulate the data instead of displaying it, see the mem2array primitives.)

$target_name mww *addr* *word*   [Command]
$target_name mwh *addr* *halfword*   [Command]
$target_name mwb *addr* *byte*   [Command]

> Writes the specified *word* (32 bits), *halfword* (16 bits), or *byte* (8-bit) pattern, at the specified address *addr*.

11.5 Target Events

At various times, certain things can happen, or you want them to happen. For example:

- What should happen when GDB connects? Should your target reset?
- When GDB tries to flash the target, do you need to enable the flash via a special command?
- Is using SRST appropriate (and possible) on your system? Or instead of that, do you need to issue JTAG commands to trigger reset? SRST usually resets everything on the scan chain, which can be inappropriate.
- During reset, do you need to write to certain memory locations to set up system clocks or to reconfigure the SDRAM? How about configuring the watchdog timer, or other peripherals, to stop running while you hold the core stopped for debugging?

All of the above items can be addressed by target event handlers. These are set up by $target_name configure -event or target create ... -event.

The programmer's model matches the -command option used in Tcl/Tk buttons and events. The two examples below act the same, but one creates and invokes a small procedure while the other inlines it.

```
proc my_attach_proc { } {
    echo "Reset..."
    reset halt
}
mychip.cpu configure -event gdb-attach my_attach_proc
mychip.cpu configure -event gdb-attach {
    echo "Reset..."
    # To make flash probe and gdb load to flash work
    # we need a reset init.
    reset init
}
```

The following target events are defined:

- **debug-halted**
  The target has halted for debug reasons (i.e.: breakpoint)

- **debug-resumed**
  The target has resumed (i.e.: gdb said run)

- **early-halted**
  Occurs early in the halt process

- **examine-start**
  Before target examine is called.

- **examine-end**
  After target examine is called with no errors.

- **gdb-attach**
  When GDB connects. This is before any communication with the target, so this can
  be used to set up the target so it is possible to probe flash. Probing flash is necessary
  during gdb connect if gdb load is to write the image to flash. Another use of the flash
  memory map is for GDB to automatically hardware/software breakpoints depending
  on whether the breakpoint is in RAM or read only memory.

- **gdb-detach**
  When GDB disconnects

- **gdb-end**
  When the target has halted and GDB is not doing anything (see early halt)

- **gdb-flash-erase-start**
  Before the GDB flash process tries to erase the flash (default is **reset init**)

- **gdb-flash-erase-end**
  After the GDB flash process has finished erasing the flash

- **gdb-flash-write-start**
  Before GDB writes to the flash

- **gdb-flash-write-end**
  After GDB writes to the flash (default is **reset halt**)

- **gdb-start**
  Before the target steps, gdb is trying to start/resume the target

- **halted**
  The target has halted

- **reset-assert-pre**
  Issued as part of `reset` processing after `reset_init` was triggered but before either SRST alone is re-asserted on the scan chain, or `reset-assert` is triggered.

- **reset-assert**
  Issued as part of `reset` processing after `reset-assert-pre` was triggered. When such a handler is present, cores which support this event will use it instead of asserting SRST. This support is essential for debugging with JTAG interfaces which don't include an SRST line (JTAG doesn't require SRST), and for selective reset on scan chains that have multiple targets.

- **reset-assert-post**
  Issued as part of `reset` processing after `reset-assert` has been triggered. or the target asserted SRST on the entire scan chain.

- **reset-deassert-pre**
  Issued as part of `reset` processing after `reset-assert-post` has been triggered.

- **reset-deassert-post**
  Issued as part of `reset` processing after `reset-deassert-pre` has been triggered and (if the target is using it) after SRST has been released on the scan chain.

- **reset-end**
  Issued as the final step in `reset` processing.

- **reset-init**
  Used by **reset init** command for board-specific initialization. This event fires after *reset-deassert-post*.

  This is where you would configure PLLs and clocking, set up DRAM so you can download programs that don't fit in on-chip SRAM, set up pin multiplexing, and so on. (You may be able to switch to a fast JTAG clock rate here, after the target clocks are fully set up.)

- **reset-start**
  Issued as part of `reset` processing before `reset_init` is called.

  This is the most robust place to use `jtag_rclk` or `adapter_khz` to switch to a low JTAG clock rate, when reset disables PLLs needed to use a fast clock.

- **resume-start**
  Before any target is resumed

- **resume-end**
  After all targets have resumed

- **resumed**
  Target has resumed

- **trace-config**
  After target hardware trace configuration was changed

12 Flash Commands

OpenOCD has different commands for NOR and NAND flash; the "flash" command works with NOR flash, while the "nand" command works with NAND flash. This partially reflects different hardware technologies: NOR flash usually supports direct CPU instruction and data bus access, while data from a NAND flash must be copied to memory before it can be used. (SPI flash must also be copied to memory before use.) However, the documentation also uses "flash" as a generic term; for example, "Put flash configuration in board-specific files".

Flash Steps:

1. Configure via the command **flash bank**
   Do this in a board-specific configuration file, passing parameters as needed by the driver.

2. Operate on the flash via **flash subcommand**
   Often commands to manipulate the flash are typed by a human, or run via a script in some automated way. Common tasks include writing a boot loader, operating system, or other data.

3. GDB Flashing
   Flashing via GDB requires the flash be configured via "flash bank", and the GDB flash features be enabled. See [GDB Configuration], page 33.

Many CPUs have the ablity to "boot" from the first flash bank. This means that mis-programming that bank can "brick" a system, so that it can't boot. JTAG tools, like OpenOCD, are often then used to "de-brick" the board by (re)installing working boot firmware.

12.1 Flash Configuration Commands

flash bank *name driver base size chip_width bus_width target*   [Config Command]
          [*driver_options*]
  Configures a flash bank which provides persistent storage for addresses from *base* to *base+size−1*. These banks will often be visible to GDB through the target's memory map. In some cases, configuring a flash bank will activate extra commands; see the driver-specific documentation.

  - *name* ... may be used to reference the flash bank in other flash commands. A number is also available.
  - *driver* ... identifies the controller driver associated with the flash bank being declared. This is usually **cfi** for external flash, or else the name of a microcontroller with embedded flash memory. See [Flash Driver List], page 72.
  - *base* ... Base address of the flash chip.
  - *size* ... Size of the chip, in bytes. For some drivers, this value is detected from the hardware.
  - *chip_width* ... Width of the flash chip, in bytes; ignored for most microcontroller drivers.
  - *bus_width* ... Width of the data bus used to access the chip, in bytes; ignored for most microcontroller drivers.

- *target* ... Names the target used to issue commands to the flash controller.
- *driver_options* ... drivers may support, or require, additional parameters. See the driver-specific documentation for more information.

> **Note:** This command is not available after OpenOCD initialization has completed. Use it in board specific configuration files, not interactively.

flash banks   [Command]
> Prints a one-line summary of each device that was declared using **flash bank**, numbered from zero. Note that this is the *plural* form; the *singular* form is a very different command.

flash list   [Command]
> Retrieves a list of associative arrays for each device that was declared using **flash bank**, numbered from zero. This returned list can be manipulated easily from within scripts.

flash probe *num*   [Command]
> Identify the flash, or validate the parameters of the configured flash. Operation depends on the flash type. The *num* parameter is a value shown by **flash banks**. Most flash commands will implicitly *autoprobe* the bank; flash drivers can distinguish between probing and autoprobing, but most don't bother.

12.2 Erasing, Reading, Writing to Flash

One feature distinguishing NOR flash from NAND or serial flash technologies is that for read access, it acts exactly like any other addressible memory. This means you can use normal memory read commands like **mdw** or **dump_image** with it, with no special **flash** subcommands. See [Memory access], page 99, and [Image access], page 100.

Write access works differently. Flash memory normally needs to be erased before it's written. Erasing a sector turns all of its bits to ones, and writing can turn ones into zeroes. This is why there are special commands for interactive erasing and writing, and why GDB needs to know which parts of the address space hold NOR flash memory.

> **Note:** Most of these erase and write commands leverage the fact that NOR flash chips consume target address space. They implicitly refer to the current JTAG target, and map from an address in that target's address space back to a flash bank. A few commands use abstract addressing based on bank and sector numbers, and don't depend on searching the current target and its address space. Avoid confusing the two command models.

Some flash chips implement software protection against accidental writes, since such buggy writes could in some cases "brick" a system. For such systems, erasing and writing may require sector protection to be disabled first. Examples include CFI flash such as "Intel Advanced Bootblock flash", and AT91SAM7 on-chip flash. See [flash protect], page 72.

flash erase_sector *num first last*   [Command]
> Erase sectors in bank *num*, starting at sector *first* up to and including *last*. Sector numbering starts at 0. Providing a *last* sector of **last** specifies "to the end of the flash bank". The *num* parameter is a value shown by **flash banks**.

flash erase_address [pad] [unlock] *address length*   [Command]
> Erase sectors starting at *address* for *length* bytes. Unless **pad** is specified, *address* must begin a flash sector, and *address* + *length* − 1 must end a sector. Specifying **pad** erases extra data at the beginning and/or end of the specified region, as needed to erase only full sectors. The flash bank to use is inferred from the *address*, and the specified length must stay within that bank. As a special case, when *length* is zero and *address* is the start of the bank, the whole flash is erased. If **unlock** is specified, then the flash is unprotected before erase starts.

flash fillw *address word length*   [Command]
flash fillh *address halfword length*   [Command]
flash fillb *address byte length*   [Command]
> Fills flash memory with the specified *word* (32 bits), *halfword* (16 bits), or *byte* (8-bit) pattern, starting at *address* and continuing for *length* units (word/halfword/byte). No erasure is done before writing; when needed, that must be done before issuing this command. Writes are done in blocks of up to 1024 bytes, and each write is verified by reading back the data and comparing it to what was written. The flash bank to use is inferred from the *address* of each block, and the specified length must stay within that bank.

flash write_bank *num filename offset*   [Command]
> Write the binary **filename** to flash bank *num*, starting at *offset* bytes from the beginning of the bank. The *num* parameter is a value shown by **flash banks**.

flash read_bank *num filename offset length*   [Command]
> Read *length* bytes from the flash bank *num* starting at *offset* and write the contents to the binary **filename**. The *num* parameter is a value shown by **flash banks**.

flash verify_bank *num filename offset*   [Command]
> Compare the contents of the binary file *filename* with the contents of the flash *num* starting at *offset*. Fails if the contents do not match. The *num* parameter is a value shown by **flash banks**.

flash write_image [erase] [unlock] *filename* [offset] [type]   [Command]
> Write the image **filename** to the current target's flash bank(s). Only loadable sections from the image are written. A relocation *offset* may be specified, in which case it is added to the base address for each section in the image. The file [type] can be specified explicitly as **bin** (binary), **ihex** (Intel hex), **elf** (ELF file), **s19** (Motorola s19). **mem**, or **builder**. The relevant flash sectors will be erased prior to programming if the **erase** parameter is given. If **unlock** is provided, then the flash banks are unlocked before erase and program. The flash bank to use is inferred from the address of each image section.
>
>> **Warning:** Be careful using the **erase** flag when the flash is holding data you want to preserve. Portions of the flash outside those described in the image's sections might be erased with no notice.
>>
>> - When a section of the image being written does not fill out all the sectors it uses, the unwritten parts of those sectors are necessarily also erased, because sectors can't be partially erased.

- Data stored in sector "holes" between image sections are also affected. For example, `"flash write_image erase ..."` of an image with one byte at the beginning of a flash bank and one byte at the end erases the entire bank – not just the two sectors being written.

  Also, when flash protection is important, you must re-apply it after it has been removed by the `unlock` flag.

12.3 Other Flash commands

`flash erase_check` *num*   [Command]
  Check erase state of sectors in flash bank *num*, and display that status. The *num* parameter is a value shown by `flash banks`.

`flash info` *num*   [Command]
  Print info about flash bank *num* The *num* parameter is a value shown by `flash banks`. This command will first query the hardware, it does not print cached and possibly stale information.

`flash protect` *num* *first* *last* (`on`|`off`)   [Command]
  Enable (`on`) or disable (`off`) protection of flash sectors in flash bank *num*, starting at sector *first* and continuing up to and including *last*. Providing a *last* sector of `last` specifies "to the end of the flash bank". The *num* parameter is a value shown by `flash banks`.

`flash padded_value` *num* *value*   [Command]
  Sets the default value used for padding any image sections, This should normally match the flash bank erased value. If not specified by this comamnd or the flash driver then it defaults to 0xff.

`program` *filename* [*verify*] [*reset*] [*exit*] [*offset*]   [Command]
  This is a helper script that simplifies using OpenOCD as a standalone programmer. The only required parameter is `filename`, the others are optional. See Chapter 13 [Flash Programming], page 94.

12.4 Flash Driver List

As noted above, the `flash bank` command requires a driver name, and allows driver-specific options and behaviors. Some drivers also activate driver-specific commands.

`virtual`   [Flash Driver]
  This is a special driver that maps a previously defined bank to another address. All bank settings will be copied from the master physical bank.

  The *virtual* driver defines one mandatory parameters,

  - *master_bank* The bank that this virtual address refers to.

  So in the following example addresses 0xbfc00000 and 0x9fc00000 refer to the flash bank defined at address 0x1fc00000. Any cmds executed on the virtual banks are actually performed on the physical banks.

```
flash bank $_FLASHNAME pic32mx 0x1fc00000 0 0 0 $_TARGETNAME
flash bank vbank0 virtual 0xbfc00000 0 0 0 $_TARGETNAME $_FLASHNAME
flash bank vbank1 virtual 0x9fc00000 0 0 0 $_TARGETNAME $_FLASHNAME
```

12.4.1 External Flash

cfi   [Flash Driver]

The "Common Flash Interface" (CFI) is the main standard for external NOR flash chips, each of which connects to a specific external chip select on the CPU. Frequently the first such chip is used to boot the system. Your board's reset-init handler might need to configure additional chip selects using other commands (like: mww to configure a bus and its timings), or perhaps configure a GPIO pin that controls the "write protect" pin on the flash chip. The CFI driver can use a target-specific working area to significantly speed up operation.

The CFI driver can accept the following optional parameters, in any order:

- *jedec_probe* ... is used to detect certain non-CFI flash ROMs, like AM29LV010 and similar types.

- *x16_as_x8* ... when a 16-bit flash is hooked up to an 8-bit bus.

To configure two adjacent banks of 16 MBytes each, both sixteen bits (two bytes) wide on a sixteen bit bus:

```
flash bank $_FLASHNAME cfi 0x00000000 0x01000000 2 2 $_TARGETNAME
flash bank $_FLASHNAME cfi 0x01000000 0x01000000 2 2 $_TARGETNAME
```

To configure one bank of 32 MBytes built from two sixteen bit (two byte) wide parts wired in parallel to create a thirty-two bit (four byte) bus with doubled throughput:

```
flash bank $_FLASHNAME cfi 0x00000000 0x02000000 2 4 $_TARGETNAME
```

jtagspi   [Flash Driver]

Several FPGAs and CPLDs can retrieve their configuration (bitstream) from a SPI flash connected to them. To access this flash from the host, the device is first programmed with a special proxy bitstream that exposes the SPI flash on the device's JTAG interface. The flash can then be accessed through JTAG.

Since signaling between JTAG and SPI is compatible, all that is required for a proxy bitstream is to connect TDI-MOSI, TDO-MISO, TCK-CLK and activate the flash chip select when the JTAG state machine is in SHIFT-DR. Such a bitstream for several Xilinx FPGAs can be found in contrib/loaders/flash/fpga/xilinx_bscan_spi.py. It requires migen (http://github.com/m-labs/migen) and a Xilinx toolchain to build.

This flash bank driver requires a target on a JTAG tap and will access that tap directly. Since no support from the target is needed, the target can be a "testee" dummy. Since the target does not expose the flash memory mapping, target commands that would otherwise be expected to access the flash will not work. These include all *_image and $target_name m* commands as well as program. Equivalent functionality is available through the flash write_bank, flash read_bank, and flash verify_bank commands.

- *ir* ... is loaded into the JTAG IR to map the flash as the JTAG DR. For the bitstreams generated from xilinx_bscan_spi.py this is the *USER1* instruction.

- *dr_length* ... is the length of the DR register. This will be 1 for `xilinx_bscan_spi.py` bitstreams and most other cases.

```
target create $_TARGETNAME testee -chain-position $_CHIPNAME.fpga
set _XILINX_USER1 0x02
set _DR_LENGTH 1
flash bank $_FLASHNAME spi 0x0 0 0 0 $_TARGETNAME $_XILINX_USER1 $_DR_LENGTH
```

`lpcspifi`   [Flash Driver]

NXP's LPC43xx and LPC18xx families include a proprietary SPI Flash Interface (SPIFI) peripheral that can drive and provide memory mapped access to external SPI flash devices.

The lpcspifi driver initializes this interface and provides program and erase functionality for these serial flash devices. Use of this driver **requires** a working area of at least 1kB to be configured on the target device; more than this will significantly reduce flash programming times.

The setup command only requires the *base* parameter. All other parameters are ignored, and the flash size and layout are configured by the driver.

```
flash bank $_FLASHNAME lpcspifi 0x14000000 0 0 0 $_TARGETNAME
```

`stmsmi`   [Flash Driver]

Some devices form STMicroelectronics (e.g. STR75x MCU family, SPEAr MPU family) include a proprietary "Serial Memory Interface" (SMI) controller able to drive external SPI flash devices. Depending on specific device and board configuration, up to 4 external flash devices can be connected.

SMI makes the flash content directly accessible in the CPU address space; each external device is mapped in a memory bank. CPU can directly read data, execute code and boot from SMI banks. Normal OpenOCD commands like `mdw` can be used to display the flash content.

The setup command only requires the *base* parameter in order to identify the memory bank. All other parameters are ignored. Additional information, like flash size, are detected automatically.

```
flash bank $_FLASHNAME stmsmi 0xf8000000 0 0 0 $_TARGETNAME
```

`mrvlqspi`   [Flash Driver]

This driver supports QSPI flash controller of Marvell's Wireless Microcontroller platform.

The flash size is autodetected based on the table of known JEDEC IDs hardcoded in the OpenOCD sources.

```
flash bank $_FLASHNAME mrvlqspi 0x0 0 0 0 $_TARGETNAME 0x46010000
```

12.4.2 Internal Flash (Microcontrollers)

`aduc702x`   [Flash Driver]

The ADUC702x analog microcontrollers from Analog Devices include internal flash and use ARM7TDMI cores. The aduc702x flash driver works with models ADUC7019 through ADUC7028. The setup command only requires the *target* argument since all devices in this family have the same memory layout.

```
flash bank $_FLASHNAME aduc702x 0 0 0 0 $_TARGETNAME
```

at91samd [Flash Driver]

at91samd chip-erase [Command]

Issues a complete Flash erase via the Device Service Unit (DSU). This can be used to erase a chip back to its factory state and does not require the processor to be halted.

at91samd set-security [Command]

Secures the Flash via the Set Security Bit (SSB) command. This prevents access to the Flash and can only be undone by using the chip-erase command which erases the Flash contents and turns off the security bit. Warning: at this time, openocd will not be able to communicate with a secured chip and it is therefore not possible to chip-erase it without using another tool.

```
at91samd set-security enable
```

at91samd eeprom [Command]

Shows or sets the EEPROM emulation size configuration, stored in the User Row of the Flash. When setting, the EEPROM size must be specified in bytes and it must be one of the permitted sizes according to the datasheet. Settings are written immediately but only take effect on MCU reset. EEPROM emulation requires additional firmware support and the minumum EEPROM size may not be the same as the minimum that the hardware supports. Set the EEPROM size to 0 in order to disable this feature.

```
at91samd eeprom
at91samd eeprom 1024
```

at91samd bootloader [Command]

Shows or sets the bootloader size configuration, stored in the User Row of the Flash. This is called the BOOTPROT region. When setting, the bootloader size must be specified in bytes and it must be one of the permitted sizes according to the datasheet. Settings are written immediately but only take effect on MCU reset. Setting the bootloader size to 0 disables bootloader protection.

```
at91samd bootloader
at91samd bootloader 16384
```

at91sam3 [Flash Driver]

All members of the AT91SAM3 microcontroller family from Atmel include internal flash and use ARM's Cortex-M3 core. The driver currently (6/22/09) recognizes the AT91SAM3U[1/2/4][C/E] chips. Note that the driver was orginaly developed and tested using the AT91SAM3U4E, using a SAM3U-EK eval board. Support for other chips in the family was cribbed from the data sheet. *Note to future readers/updaters: Please remove this worrysome comment after other chips are confirmed.*

The AT91SAM3U4[E/C] (256K) chips have two flash banks; most other chips have one flash bank. In all cases the flash banks are at the following fixed locations:

```
# Flash bank 0 - all chips
flash bank $_FLASHNAME at91sam3 0x00080000 0 1 1 $_TARGETNAME
```

```
# Flash bank 1 - only 256K chips
flash bank $_FLASHNAME at91sam3 0x00100000 0 1 1 $_TARGETNAME
```

Internally, the AT91SAM3 flash memory is organized as follows. Unlike the AT91SAM7 chips, these are not used as parameters to the **flash bank** command:

- *N-Banks:* 256K chips have 2 banks, others have 1 bank.
- *Bank Size:* 128K/64K Per flash bank
- *Sectors:* 16 or 8 per bank
- *SectorSize:* 8K Per Sector
- *PageSize:* 256 bytes per page. Note that OpenOCD operates on 'sector' sizes, not page sizes.

The AT91SAM3 driver adds some additional commands:

at91sam3 gpnvm   [Command]
at91sam3 gpnvm clear *number*   [Command]
at91sam3 gpnvm set *number*   [Command]
at91sam3 gpnvm show [all|*number*]   [Command]

> With no parameters, **show** or **show all**, shows the status of all GPNVM bits. With **show** *number*, displays that bit.
>
> With **set** *number* or **clear** *number*, modifies that GPNVM bit.

at91sam3 info   [Command]

> This command attempts to display information about the AT91SAM3 chip. *First* it read the **CHIPID_CIDR** [address 0x400e0740, see Section 28.2.1, page 505 of the AT91SAM3U 29/may/2009 datasheet, document id: doc6430A] and decodes the values. *Second* it reads the various clock configuration registers and attempts to display how it believes the chip is configured. By default, the SLOWCLK is assumed to be 32768 Hz, see the command **at91sam3 slowclk**.

at91sam3 slowclk [*value*]   [Command]

> This command shows/sets the slow clock frequency used in the **at91sam3 info** command calculations above.

at91sam4   [Flash Driver]

> All members of the AT91SAM4 microcontroller family from Atmel include internal flash and use ARM's Cortex-M4 core. This driver uses the same cmd names/syntax as See [at91sam3], page 75.

at91sam4l   [Flash Driver]

> All members of the AT91SAM4L microcontroller family from Atmel include internal flash and use ARM's Cortex-M4 core. This driver uses the same cmd names/syntax as See [at91sam3], page 75.

The AT91SAM4L driver adds some additional commands:

at91sam4l smap_reset_deassert   [Command]

> This command releases internal reset held by SMAP and prepares reset vector catch in case of reset halt. Command is used internally in event event reset-deassert-post.

at91sam7   [Flash Driver]

All members of the AT91SAM7 microcontroller family from Atmel include internal flash and use ARM7TDMI cores. The driver automatically recognizes a number of these chips using the chip identification register, and autoconfigures itself.

> `flash bank $_FLASHNAME at91sam7 0 0 0 0 $_TARGETNAME`

For chips which are not recognized by the controller driver, you must provide additional parameters in the following order:

- *chip_model* ... label used with `flash info`
- *banks*
- *sectors_per_bank*
- *pages_per_sector*
- *pages_size*
- *num_nvm_bits*
- *freq_khz* ... required if an external clock is provided, optional (but recommended) when the oscillator frequency is known

It is recommended that you provide zeroes for all of those values except the clock frequency, so that everything except that frequency will be autoconfigured. Knowing the frequency helps ensure correct timings for flash access.

The flash controller handles erases automatically on a page (128/256 byte) basis, so explicit erase commands are not necessary for flash programming. However, there is an "EraseAll" command that can erase an entire flash plane (of up to 256KB), and it will be used automatically when you issue `flash erase_sector` or `flash erase_address` commands.

at91sam7 gpnvm *bitnum* (`set`|`clear`)   [Command]

Set or clear a "General Purpose Non-Volatile Memory" (GPNVM) bit for the processor. Each processor has a number of such bits, used for controlling features such as brownout detection (so they are not truly general purpose).

> **Note:** This assumes that the first flash bank (number 0) is associated with the appropriate at91sam7 target.

avr   [Flash Driver]

The AVR 8-bit microcontrollers from Atmel integrate flash memory. *The current implementation is incomplete.*

efm32   [Flash Driver]

All members of the EFM32 microcontroller family from Energy Micro include internal flash and use ARM Cortex M3 cores. The driver automatically recognizes a number of these chips using the chip identification register, and autoconfigures itself.

> `flash bank $_FLASHNAME efm32 0 0 0 0 $_TARGETNAME`

The current implementation is incomplete. Unprotecting flash pages is not supported.

lpc2000   [Flash Driver]

This is the driver to support internal flash of all members of the LPC11(x)00 and LPC1300 microcontroller families and most members of the LPC800, LPC1500,

LPC1700, LPC1800, LPC2000, LPC4000 and LPC54100 microcontroller families from NXP.

> **Note:** There are LPC2000 devices which are not supported by the *lpc2000* driver: The LPC2888 is supported by the *lpc288x* driver. The LPC29xx family is supported by the *lpc2900* driver.

The *lpc2000* driver defines two mandatory and one optional parameters, which must appear in the following order:

- *variant* ...   required, may be `lpc2000_v1` (older LPC21xx and LPC22xx) `lpc2000_v2` (LPC213x, LPC214x, LPC210[123], LPC23xx and LPC24xx) `lpc1700` (LPC175x and LPC176x and LPC177x/8x) `lpc4300` - available also as `lpc1800` alias (LPC18x[2357] and LPC43x[2357]) `lpc800` (LPC8xx) `lpc1100` (LPC11(x)xx and LPC13xx) `lpc1500` (LPC15xx) `lpc54100` (LPC541xx) `lpc4000` (LPC40xx) or `auto` - automatically detects flash variant and size for LPC11(x)00, LPC8xx, LPC13xx, LPC17xx and LPC40xx

- *clock_kHz* ... the frequency, in kiloHertz, at which the core is running

- `calc_checksum` ... optional (but you probably want to provide this!), telling the driver to calculate a valid checksum for the exception vector table.

  > **Note:** If you don't provide `calc_checksum` when you're writing the vector table, the boot ROM will almost certainly ignore your flash image. However, if you do provide it, with most tool chains `verify_image` will fail.

LPC flashes don't require the chip and bus width to be specified.

```
flash bank $_FLASHNAME lpc2000 0x0 0x7d000 0 0 $_TARGETNAME \
    lpc2000_v2 14765 calc_checksum
```

`lpc2000 part_id` bank   [Command]
Displays the four byte part identifier associated with the specified flash *bank*.

`lpc288x`   [Flash Driver]
The LPC2888 microcontroller from NXP needs slightly different flash support from its lpc2000 siblings. The *lpc288x* driver defines one mandatory parameter, the programming clock rate in Hz. LPC flashes don't require the chip and bus width to be specified.

```
flash bank $_FLASHNAME lpc288x 0 0 0 0 $_TARGETNAME 12000000
```

`lpc2900`   [Flash Driver]
This driver supports the LPC29xx ARM968E based microcontroller family from NXP.

The predefined parameters *base*, *size*, *chip_width* and *bus_width* of the **flash bank** command are ignored. Flash size and sector layout are auto-configured by the driver. The driver has one additional mandatory parameter: The CPU clock rate (in kHz) at the time the flash operations will take place. Most of the time this will not be the crystal frequency, but a higher PLL frequency. The **reset-init** event handler in the board script is usually the place where you start the PLL.

The driver rejects flashless devices (currently the LPC2930).

The EEPROM in LPC2900 devices is not mapped directly into the address space. It must be handled much more like NAND flash memory, and will therefore be handled by a separate `lpc2900_eeprom` driver (not yet available).

Sector protection in terms of the LPC2900 is handled transparently. Every time a sector needs to be erased or programmed, it is automatically unprotected. What is shown as protection status in the **flash info** command, is actually the LPC2900 *sector security*. This is a mechanism to prevent a sector from ever being erased or programmed again. As this is an irreversible mechanism, it is handled by a special command (`lpc2900 secure_sector`), and not by the standard **flash protect** command.

Example for a 125 MHz clock frequency:

```
flash bank $_FLASHNAME lpc2900 0 0 0 0 $_TARGETNAME 125000
```

Some `lpc2900`-specific commands are defined. In the following command list, the *bank* parameter is the bank number as obtained by the **flash banks** command.

lpc2900 signature *bank*   [Command]
    Calculates a 128-bit hash value, the *signature*, from the whole flash content. This is a hardware feature of the flash block, hence the calculation is very fast. You may use this to verify the content of a programmed device against a known signature. Example:

```
lpc2900 signature 0
  signature: 0x5f40cdc8:0xc64e592e:0x10490f89:0x32a0f317
```

lpc2900 read_custom *bank filename*   [Command]
    Reads the 912 bytes of customer information from the flash index sector, and saves it to a file in binary format. Example:

```
lpc2900 read_custom 0 /path_to/customer_info.bin
```

The index sector of the flash is a *write-only* sector. It cannot be erased! In order to guard against unintentional write access, all following commands need to be preceeded by a successful call to the **password** command:

lpc2900 password *bank password*   [Command]
    You need to use this command right before each of the following commands: `lpc2900 write_custom`, `lpc2900 secure_sector`, `lpc2900 secure_jtag`.

    The password string is fixed to "I_know_what_I_am_doing". Example:

```
lpc2900 password 0 I_know_what_I_am_doing
  Potentially dangerous operation allowed in next command!
```

lpc2900 write_custom *bank filename type*   [Command]
    Writes the content of the file into the customer info space of the flash index sector. The filetype can be specified with the *type* field. Possible values for *type* are: *bin* (binary), *ihex* (Intel hex format), *elf* (ELF binary) or *s19* (Motorola S-records). The file must contain a single section, and the contained data length must be exactly 912 bytes.

    Attention: This cannot be reverted! Be careful!

Example:

```
lpc2900 write_custom 0 /path_to/customer_info.bin bin
```

lpc2900 secure_sector *bank first last*   [Command]
> Secures the sector range from *first* to *last* (including) against further program
> and erase operations. The sector security will be effective after the next power
> cycle.
>
> **Attention:** This cannot be reverted! Be careful!

Secured sectors appear as *protected* in the **flash info** command. Example:

```
lpc2900 secure_sector 0 1 1
flash info 0
  #0 : lpc2900 at 0x20000000, size 0x000c0000, (...)
          #  0: 0x00000000 (0x2000 8kB) not protected
          #  1: 0x00002000 (0x2000 8kB) protected
          #  2: 0x00004000 (0x2000 8kB) not protected
```

lpc2900 secure_jtag *bank*   [Command]
> Irreversibly disable the JTAG port. The new JTAG security setting will be
> effective after the next power cycle.
>
> **Attention:** This cannot be reverted! Be careful!

Examples:

```
lpc2900 secure_jtag 0
```

ocl   [Flash Driver]
> This driver is an implementation of the "on chip flash loader" protocol proposed by
> Pavel Chromy.
>
> It is a minimalistic command-response protocol intended to be used over a
> DCC when communicating with an internal or external flash loader running
> from RAM. An example implementation for AT91SAM7x is available in
> contrib/loaders/flash/at91sam7x/.

```
flash bank $_FLASHNAME ocl 0 0 0 0 $_TARGETNAME
```

pic32mx   [Flash Driver]
> The PIC32MX microcontrollers are based on the MIPS 4K cores, and integrate flash
> memory.

```
flash bank $_FLASHNAME pix32mx 0x1fc00000 0 0 0 $_TARGETNAME
flash bank $_FLASHNAME pix32mx 0x1d000000 0 0 0 $_TARGETNAME
```

Some pic32mx-specific commands are defined:

pic32mx pgm_word *address value bank*   [Command]
> Programs the specified 32-bit *value* at the given *address* in the specified chip
> *bank*.

pic32mx unlock *bank*   [Command]
> Unlock and erase specified chip *bank*. This will remove any Code Protection.

psoc4 [Flash Driver]

All members of the PSoC 41xx/42xx microcontroller family from Cypress include internal flash and use ARM Cortex M0 cores. The driver automatically recognizes a number of these chips using the chip identification register, and autoconfigures itself.

Note: Erased internal flash reads as 00. System ROM of PSoC 4 does not implement erase of a flash sector.

```
flash bank $_FLASHNAME psoc4 0 0 0 0 $_TARGETNAME
```

psoc4-specific commands

psoc4 flash_autoerase *num* (*on*|*off*) [Command]

Enables or disables autoerase mode for a flash bank.

If flash_autoerase is off, use mass_erase before flash programming. Flash erase command fails if region to erase is not whole flash memory.

If flash_autoerase is on, a sector is both erased and programmed in one system ROM call. Flash erase command is ignored. This mode is suitable for gdb load.

The *num* parameter is a value shown by **flash banks**.

psoc4 mass_erase *num* [Command]

Erases the contents of the flash memory, protection and security lock.

The *num* parameter is a value shown by **flash banks**.

stellaris [Flash Driver]

All members of the Stellaris LM3Sxxx, LM4x and Tiva C microcontroller families from Texas Instruments include internal flash. The driver automatically recognizes a number of these chips using the chip identification register, and autoconfigures itself.[1]

```
flash bank $_FLASHNAME stellaris 0 0 0 0 $_TARGETNAME
```

stellaris recover [Command]

Performs the *Recovering a "Locked" Device* procedure to restore the flash and its associated nonvolatile registers to their factory default values (erased). This is the only way to remove flash protection or re-enable debugging if that capability has been disabled.

Note that the final "power cycle the chip" step in this procedure must be performed by hand, since OpenOCD can't do it.

> **Warning:** if more than one Stellaris chip is connected, the procedure is applied to all of them.

stm32f1x [Flash Driver]

All members of the STM32F0, STM32F1 and STM32F3 microcontroller families from ST Microelectronics include internal flash and use ARM Cortex-M0/M3/M4 cores. The driver automatically recognizes a number of these chips using the chip identification register, and autoconfigures itself.

---

[1] Currently there is a **stellaris mass_erase** command. That seems pointless since the same effect can be had using the standard **flash erase_address** command.

```
flash bank $_FLASHNAME stm32f1x 0 0 0 0 $_TARGETNAME
```

Note that some devices have been found that have a flash size register that contains an invalid value, to workaround this issue you can override the probed value used by the flash driver.

```
flash bank $_FLASHNAME stm32f1x 0 0x20000 0 0 $_TARGETNAME
```

If you have a target with dual flash banks then define the second bank as per the following example.

```
flash bank $_FLASHNAME stm32f1x 0x08080000 0 0 0 $_TARGETNAME
```

Some stm32f1x-specific commands[2] are defined:

stm32f1x lock *num*   [Command]
> Locks the entire stm32 device. The *num* parameter is a value shown by **flash banks**.

stm32f1x unlock *num*   [Command]
> Unlocks the entire stm32 device. The *num* parameter is a value shown by **flash banks**.

stm32f1x options_read *num*   [Command]
> Read and display the stm32 option bytes written by the **stm32f1x options_write** command. The *num* parameter is a value shown by **flash banks**.

stm32f1x options_write *num* **(SWWDG|HWWDG)**   [Command]
> **(RSTSTNDBY|NORSTSTNDBY) (RSTSTOP|NORSTSTOP)**
> Writes the stm32 option byte with the specified values. The *num* parameter is a value shown by **flash banks**.

stm32f2x   [Flash Driver]
> All members of the STM32F2 and STM32F4 microcontroller families from ST Microelectronics include internal flash and use ARM Cortex-M3/M4 cores. The driver automatically recognizes a number of these chips using the chip identification register, and autoconfigures itself.
>
> Note that some devices have been found that have a flash size register that contains an invalid value, to workaround this issue you can override the probed value used by the flash driver.
>
> ```
> flash bank $_FLASHNAME stm32f2x 0 0x20000 0 0 $_TARGETNAME
> ```
>
> Some stm32f2x-specific commands are defined:

stm32f2x lock *num*   [Command]
> Locks the entire stm32 device. The *num* parameter is a value shown by **flash banks**.

stm32f2x unlock *num*   [Command]
> Unlocks the entire stm32 device. The *num* parameter is a value shown by **flash banks**.

---

[2] Currently there is a **stm32f1x mass_erase** command. That seems pointless since the same effect can be had using the standard **flash erase_address** command.

`stm32lx`   [Flash Driver]

All members of the STM32L microcontroller families from ST Microelectronics include internal flash and use ARM Cortex-M3 and Cortex-M0+ cores. The driver automatically recognizes a number of these chips using the chip identification register, and autoconfigures itself.

Note that some devices have been found that have a flash size register that contains an invalid value, to workaround this issue you can override the probed value used by the flash driver. If you use 0 as the bank base address, it tells the driver to autodetect the bank location assuming you're configuring the second bank.

```
flash bank $_FLASHNAME stm32lx 0x08000000 0x20000 0 0 $_TARGETNAME
```

Some stm32lx-specific commands are defined:

stm32lx mass_erase *num*   [Command]

Mass erases the entire stm32lx device (all flash banks and EEPROM data). This is the only way to unlock a protected flash (unless RDP Level is 2 which can't be unlocked at all). The *num* parameter is a value shown by **flash banks**.

`str7x`   [Flash Driver]

All members of the STR7 microcontroller family from ST Microelectronics include internal flash and use ARM7TDMI cores. The *str7x* driver defines one mandatory parameter, *variant*, which is either **STR71x**, **STR73x** or **STR75x**.

```
flash bank $_FLASHNAME str7x \
     0x40000000 0x00040000 0 0 $_TARGETNAME STR71x
```

str7x disable_jtag *bank*   [Command]

Activate the Debug/Readout protection mechanism for the specified flash bank.

`str9x`   [Flash Driver]

Most members of the STR9 microcontroller family from ST Microelectronics include internal flash and use ARM966E cores. The str9 needs the flash controller to be configured using the **str9x flash_config** command prior to Flash programming.

```
flash bank $_FLASHNAME str9x 0x40000000 0x00040000 0 0 $_TARGETNAME
str9x flash_config 0 4 2 0 0x80000
```

str9x flash_config *num bbsr nbbsr bbadr nbbadr*   [Command]

Configures the str9 flash controller. The *num* parameter is a value shown by **flash banks**.

- *bbsr* - Boot Bank Size register
- *nbbsr* - Non Boot Bank Size register
- *bbadr* - Boot Bank Start Address register
- *nbbadr* - Boot Bank Start Address register

`str9xpec`   [Flash Driver]

Only use this driver for locking/unlocking the device or configuring the option bytes. Use the standard str9 driver for programming. Before using the flash commands the turbo mode must be enabled using the **str9xpec enable_turbo** command.

Here is some background info to help you better understand how this driver works. OpenOCD has two flash drivers for the str9:

1. Standard driver **str9x** programmed via the str9 core. Normally used for flash programming as it is faster than the **str9xpec** driver.

2. Direct programming **str9xpec** using the flash controller. This is an ISC compliant (IEEE 1532) tap connected in series with the str9 core. The str9 core does not need to be running to program using this flash driver. Typical use for this driver is locking/unlocking the target and programming the option bytes.

Before we run any commands using the **str9xpec** driver we must first disable the str9 core. This example assumes the **str9xpec** driver has been configured for flash bank 0.

```
# assert srst, we do not want core running
# while accessing str9xpec flash driver
jtag_reset 0 1
# turn off target polling
poll off
# disable str9 core
str9xpec enable_turbo 0
# read option bytes
str9xpec options_read 0
# re-enable str9 core
str9xpec disable_turbo 0
poll on
reset halt
```

The above example will read the str9 option bytes. When performing a unlock remember that you will not be able to halt the str9 - it has been locked. Halting the core is not required for the **str9xpec** driver as mentioned above, just issue the commands above manually or from a telnet prompt.

Several str9xpec-specific commands are defined:

str9xpec disable_turbo *num*   [Command]
    Restore the str9 into JTAG chain.

str9xpec enable_turbo *num*   [Command]
    Enable turbo mode, will simply remove the str9 from the chain and talk directly to the embedded flash controller.

str9xpec lock *num*   [Command]
    Lock str9 device. The str9 will only respond to an unlock command that will erase the device.

str9xpec part_id *num*   [Command]
    Prints the part identifier for bank *num*.

str9xpec options_cmap *num* (bank0|bank1)   [Command]
    Configure str9 boot bank.

str9xpec options_lvdsel *num* (vdd|vdd_vddq)   [Command]
    Configure str9 lvd source.

str9xpec options_lvdthd *num* (2.4v|2.7v)   [Command]
>   Configure str9 lvd threshold.

str9xpec options_lvdwarn *bank* (vdd|vdd_vddq)   [Command]
>   Configure str9 lvd reset warning source.

str9xpec options_read *num*   [Command]
>   Read str9 option bytes.

str9xpec options_write *num*   [Command]
>   Write str9 option bytes.

str9xpec unlock *num*   [Command]
>   unlock str9 device.

tms470   [Flash Driver]
>   Most members of the TMS470 microcontroller family from Texas Instruments include internal flash and use ARM7TDMI cores. This driver doesn't require the chip and bus width to be specified.
>
>   Some tms470-specific commands are defined:

tms470 flash_keyset *key0 key1 key2 key3*   [Command]
>   Saves programming keys in a register, to enable flash erase and write commands.

tms470 osc_mhz *clock_mhz*   [Command]
>   Reports the clock speed, which is used to calculate timings.

tms470 plldis (*0*|*1*)   [Command]
>   Disables (*1*) or enables (*0*) use of the PLL to speed up the flash clock.

fm3   [Flash Driver]
>   All members of the FM3 microcontroller family from Fujitsu include internal flash and use ARM Cortex M3 cores. The *fm3* driver uses the *target* parameter to select the correct bank config, it can currently be one of the following: `mb9bfxx1.cpu`, `mb9bfxx2.cpu`, `mb9bfxx3.cpu`, `mb9bfxx4.cpu`, `mb9bfxx5.cpu` or `mb9bfxx6.cpu`.
>
>   `flash bank $_FLASHNAME fm3 0 0 0 0 $_TARGETNAME`

sim3x   [Flash Driver]
>   All members of the SiM3 microcontroller family from Silicon Laboratories include internal flash and use ARM Cortex M3 cores. It supports both JTAG and SWD interface. The *sim3x* driver tries to probe the device to auto detect the MCU. If this failes, it will use the *size* parameter as the size of flash bank.
>
>   `flash bank $_FLASHNAME sim3x 0 $_CPUROMSIZE 0 0 $_TARGETNAME`
>
>   There are 2 commands defined in the *sim3x* driver:

sim3x mass_erase   [Command]
>   Erases the complete flash. This is used to unlock the flash. And this command is only possible when using the SWD interface.

sim3x lock   [Command]
>   Lock the flash. To unlock use the **sim3x mass_erase** command.

nrf51   [Flash Driver]

All members of the nRF51 microcontroller families from Nordic Semiconductor include internal flash and use ARM Cortex-M0 core.

```
flash bank $_FLASHNAME nrf51 0 0x00000000 0 0 $_TARGETNAME
```

Some nrf51-specific commands are defined:

nrf51 mass_erase   [Command]

Erases the contents of the code memory and user information configuration registers as well. It must be noted that this command works only for chips that do not have factory pre-programmed region 0 code.

mdr   [Flash Driver]

This drivers handles the integrated NOR flash on Milandr Cortex-M based controllers. A known limitation is that the Info memory can't be read or verified as it's not memory mapped.

```
flash bank <name> mdr <base> <size> \
        0 0 <target#> type page_count sec_count
```

- *type* - 0 for main memory, 1 for info memory
- *page_count* - total number of pages
- *sec_count* - number of sector per page count

Example usage:

```
if { [info exists IMEMORY] && [string equal $IMEMORY true] } {
    flash bank ${_CHIPNAME}_info.flash mdr 0x00000000 0x01000 \
        0 0 $_TARGETNAME 1 1 4
} else {
    flash bank $_CHIPNAME.flash mdr 0x00000000 0x20000 \
        0 0 $_TARGETNAME 0 32 4
}
```

12.5 NAND Flash Commands

Compared to NOR or SPI flash, NAND devices are inexpensive and high density. Today's NAND chips, and multi-chip modules, commonly hold multiple GigaBytes of data.

NAND chips consist of a number of "erase blocks" of a given size (such as 128 KBytes), each of which is divided into a number of pages (of perhaps 512 or 2048 bytes each). Each page of a NAND flash has an "out of band" (OOB) area to hold Error Correcting Code (ECC) and other metadata, usually 16 bytes of OOB for every 512 bytes of page data.

One key characteristic of NAND flash is that its error rate is higher than that of NOR flash. In normal operation, that ECC is used to correct and detect errors. However, NAND blocks can also wear out and become unusable; those blocks are then marked "bad". NAND chips are even shipped from the manufacturer with a few bad blocks. The highest density chips use a technology (MLC) that wears out more quickly, so ECC support is increasingly important as a way to detect blocks that have begun to fail, and help to preserve data integrity with techniques such as wear leveling.

Software is used to manage the ECC. Some controllers don't support ECC directly; in those cases, software ECC is used. Other controllers speed up the ECC calculations with hardware. Single-bit error correction hardware is routine. Controllers geared for newer MLC chips may correct 4 or more errors for every 512 bytes of data.

You will need to make sure that any data you write using OpenOCD includes the appropriate kind of ECC. For example, that may mean passing the `oob_softecc` flag when writing NAND data, or ensuring that the correct hardware ECC mode is used.

The basic steps for using NAND devices include:

1. Declare via the command **nand device**
   Do this in a board-specific configuration file, passing parameters as needed by the controller.
2. Configure each device using **nand probe**.
   Do this only after the associated target is set up, such as in its reset-init script or in procures defined to access that device.
3. Operate on the flash via **nand subcommand**
   Often commands to manipulate the flash are typed by a human, or run via a script in some automated way. Common task include writing a boot loader, operating system, or other data needed to initialize or de-brick a board.

NOTE: At the time this text was written, the largest NAND flash fully supported by OpenOCD is 2 GiBytes (16 GiBits). This is because the variables used to hold offsets and lengths are only 32 bits wide. (Larger chips may work in some cases, unless an offset or length is larger than 0xffffffff, the largest 32-bit unsigned integer.) Some larger devices will work, since they are actually multi-chip modules with two smaller chips and individual chipselect lines.

12.5.1 NAND Configuration Commands

NAND chips must be declared in configuration scripts, plus some additional configuration that's done after OpenOCD has initialized.

nand device *name driver target* [*configparams...*]   [Config Command]
> Declares a NAND device, which can be read and written to after it has been configured through **nand probe**. In OpenOCD, devices are single chips; this is unlike some operating systems, which may manage multiple chips as if they were a single (larger) device. In some cases, configuring a device will activate extra commands; see the controller-specific documentation.
>
> **NOTE:** This command is not available after OpenOCD initialization has completed. Use it in board specific configuration files, not interactively.
>
> - *name* ... may be used to reference the NAND bank in most other NAND commands. A number is also available.
> - *driver* ... identifies the NAND controller driver associated with the NAND device being declared. See [NAND Driver List], page 90.
> - *target* ... names the target used when issuing commands to the NAND controller.
> - *configparams* ... controllers may support, or require, additional parameters. See the controller-specific documentation for more information.

nand list   [Command]
> Prints a summary of each device declared using **nand device**, numbered from zero. Note that un-probed devices show no details.

```
> nand list
#0: NAND 1GiB 3,3V 8-bit (Micron) pagesize: 2048, buswidth: 8,
        blocksize: 131072, blocks: 8192
#1: NAND 1GiB 3,3V 8-bit (Micron) pagesize: 2048, buswidth: 8,
        blocksize: 131072, blocks: 8192
>
```

nand probe *num*   [Command]

Probes the specified device to determine key characteristics like its page and block sizes, and how many blocks it has. The *num* parameter is the value shown by **nand list**. You must (successfully) probe a device before you can use it with most other NAND commands.

12.5.2 Erasing, Reading, Writing to NAND Flash

nand dump *num filename offset length* [*oob_option*]   [Command]

Reads binary data from the NAND device and writes it to the file, starting at the specified offset. The *num* parameter is the value shown by **nand list**.

Use a complete path name for *filename*, so you don't depend on the directory used to start the OpenOCD server.

The *offset* and *length* must be exact multiples of the device's page size. They describe a data region; the OOB data associated with each such page may also be accessed.

NOTE: At the time this text was written, no error correction was done on the data that's read, unless raw access was disabled and the underlying NAND controller driver had a **read_page** method which handled that error correction.

By default, only page data is saved to the specified file. Use an *oob_option* parameter to save OOB data:

- no oob_* parameter
  Output file holds only page data; OOB is discarded.

- oob_raw
  Output file interleaves page data and OOB data; the file will be longer than "length" by the size of the spare areas associated with each data page. Note that this kind of "raw" access is different from what's implied by **nand raw_access**, which just controls whether a hardware-aware access method is used.

- oob_only
  Output file has only raw OOB data, and will be smaller than "length" since it will contain only the spare areas associated with each data page.

nand erase *num* [*offset length*]   [Command]

Erases blocks on the specified NAND device, starting at the specified *offset* and continuing for *length* bytes. Both of those values must be exact multiples of the device's block size, and the region they specify must fit entirely in the chip. If those parameters are not specified, the whole NAND chip will be erased. The *num* parameter is the value shown by **nand list**.

NOTE: This command will try to erase bad blocks, when told to do so, which will probably invalidate the manufacturer's bad block marker. For the remainder of the current server session, **nand info** will still report that the block "is" bad.

nand write *num filename offset* [*option...*]   [Command]
> Writes binary data from the file into the specified NAND device, starting at the specified offset. Those pages should already have been erased; you can't change zero bits to one bits. The *num* parameter is the value shown by **nand list**.
>
> Use a complete path name for *filename*, so you don't depend on the directory used to start the OpenOCD server.
>
> The *offset* must be an exact multiple of the device's page size. All data in the file will be written, assuming it doesn't run past the end of the device. Only full pages are written, and any extra space in the last page will be filled with 0xff bytes. (That includes OOB data, if that's being written.)
>
> **NOTE:** At the time this text was written, bad blocks are ignored. That is, this routine will not skip bad blocks, but will instead try to write them. This can cause problems.
>
> Provide at most one *option* parameter. With some NAND drivers, the meanings of these parameters may change if **nand raw_access** was used to disable hardware ECC.
>
> - no oob_* parameter
>   File has only page data, which is written. If raw acccess is in use, the OOB area will not be written. Otherwise, if the underlying NAND controller driver has a **write_page** routine, that routine may write the OOB with hardware-computed ECC data.
>
> - oob_only
>   File has only raw OOB data, which is written to the OOB area. Each page's data area stays untouched. *This can be a dangerous option*, since it can invalidate the ECC data. You may need to force raw access to use this mode.
>
> - oob_raw
>   File interleaves data and OOB data, both of which are written If raw access is enabled, the data is written first, then the un-altered OOB. Otherwise, if the underlying NAND controller driver has a **write_page** routine, that routine may modify the OOB before it's written, to include hardware-computed ECC data.
>
> - oob_softecc
>   File has only page data, which is written. The OOB area is filled with 0xff, except for a standard 1-bit software ECC code stored in conventional locations. You might need to force raw access to use this mode, to prevent the underlying driver from applying hardware ECC.
>
> - oob_softecc_kw
>   File has only page data, which is written. The OOB area is filled with 0xff, except for a 4-bit software ECC specific to the boot ROM in Marvell Kirkwood SoCs. You might need to force raw access to use this mode, to prevent the underlying driver from applying hardware ECC.

nand verify *num filename offset* [*option...*]   [Command]
> Verify the binary data in the file has been programmed to the specified NAND device, starting at the specified offset. The *num* parameter is the value shown by **nand list**.
>
> Use a complete path name for *filename*, so you don't depend on the directory used to start the OpenOCD server.

The *offset* must be an exact multiple of the device's page size. All data in the file will be read and compared to the contents of the flash, assuming it doesn't run past the end of the device. As with **nand write**, only full pages are verified, so any extra space in the last page will be filled with 0xff bytes.

The same *options* accepted by **nand write**, and the file will be processed similarly to produce the buffers that can be compared against the contents produced from **nand dump**.

NOTE: This will not work when the underlying NAND controller driver's **write_page** routine must update the OOB with a hardware-computed ECC before the data is written. This limitation may be removed in a future release.

12.5.3 Other NAND commands

nand check_bad_blocks *num* [*offset length*]   [Command]
Checks for manufacturer bad block markers on the specified NAND device. If no parameters are provided, checks the whole device; otherwise, starts at the specified *offset* and continues for *length* bytes. Both of those values must be exact multiples of the device's block size, and the region they specify must fit entirely in the chip. The *num* parameter is the value shown by **nand list**.

NOTE: Before using this command you should force raw access with **nand raw_access enable** to ensure that the underlying driver will not try to apply hardware ECC.

nand info *num*   [Command]
The *num* parameter is the value shown by **nand list**. This prints the one-line summary from "nand list", plus for devices which have been probed this also prints any known status for each block.

nand raw_access *num* (enable|disable)   [Command]
Sets or clears an flag affecting how page I/O is done. The *num* parameter is the value shown by **nand list**.

This flag is cleared (disabled) by default, but changing that value won't affect all NAND devices. The key factor is whether the underlying driver provides **read_page** or **write_page** methods. If it doesn't provide those methods, the setting of this flag is irrelevant; all access is effectively "raw".

When those methods exist, they are normally used when reading data (**nand dump** or reading bad block markers) or writing it (**nand write**). However, enabling raw access (setting the flag) prevents use of those methods, bypassing hardware ECC logic. *This can be a dangerous option*, since writing blocks with the wrong ECC data can cause them to be marked as bad.

12.5.4 NAND Driver List

As noted above, the **nand device** command allows driver-specific options and behaviors. Some controllers also activate controller-specific commands.

at91sam9   [NAND Driver]
This driver handles the NAND controllers found on AT91SAM9 family chips from Atmel. It takes two extra parameters: address of the NAND chip; address of the ECC controller.

nand device $NANDFLASH at91sam9 $CHIPNAME 0x40000000 0xffffffe800

AT91SAM9 chips support single-bit ECC hardware. The `write_page` and `read_page` methods are used to utilize the ECC hardware unless they are disabled by using the `nand raw_access` command. There are four additional commands that are needed to fully configure the AT91SAM9 NAND controller. Two are optional; most boards use the same wiring for ALE/CLE:

at91sam9 cle *num addr_line*   [Command]
> Configure the address line used for latching commands. The *num* parameter is the value shown by `nand list`.

at91sam9 ale *num addr_line*   [Command]
> Configure the address line used for latching addresses. The *num* parameter is the value shown by `nand list`.

For the next two commands, it is assumed that the pins have already been properly configured for input or output.

at91sam9 rdy_busy *num pio_base_addr pin*   [Command]
> Configure the RDY/nBUSY input from the NAND device. The *num* parameter is the value shown by `nand list`. *pio_base_addr* is the base address of the PIO controller and *pin* is the pin number.

at91sam9 ce *num pio_base_addr pin*   [Command]
> Configure the chip enable input to the NAND device. The *num* parameter is the value shown by `nand list`. *pio_base_addr* is the base address of the PIO controller and *pin* is the pin number.

davinci   [NAND Driver]
> This driver handles the NAND controllers found on DaVinci family chips from Texas Instruments. It takes three extra parameters: address of the NAND chip; hardware ECC mode to use (`hwecc1`, `hwecc4`, `hwecc4_infix`); address of the AEMIF controller on this processor.
>
> nand device davinci dm355.arm 0x02000000 hwecc4 0x01e10000
>
> All DaVinci processors support the single-bit ECC hardware, and newer ones also support the four-bit ECC hardware. The `write_page` and `read_page` methods are used to implement those ECC modes, unless they are disabled using the `nand raw_access` command.

lpc3180   [NAND Driver]
> These controllers require an extra `nand device` parameter: the clock rate used by the controller.

lpc3180 select *num [mlc|slc]*   [Command]
> Configures use of the MLC or SLC controller mode. MLC implies use of hardware ECC. The *num* parameter is the value shown by `nand list`.

At this writing, this driver includes `write_page` and `read_page` methods. Using `nand raw_access` to disable those methods will prevent use of hardware ECC in the MLC controller mode, but won't change SLC behavior.

mx3   [NAND Driver]
> This driver handles the NAND controller in i.MX31. The mxc driver should work for
> this chip aswell.

mxc   [NAND Driver]
> This driver handles the NAND controller found in Freescale i.MX chips. It has support
> for v1 (i.MX27 and i.MX31) and v2 (i.MX35). The driver takes 3 extra arguments,
> chip (mx27, mx31, mx35), ecc (noecc, hwecc) and optionally if bad block information
> should be swapped between main area and spare area (biswap), defaults to off.
>
> ```
> nand device mx35.nand mxc imx35.cpu mx35 hwecc biswap
> ```

> mxc biswap *bank_num* [*enable*|*disable*]   [Command]
> > Turns on/off bad block information swaping from main area, without parameter
> > query status.

orion   [NAND Driver]
> These controllers require an extra **nand device** parameter: the address of the con-
> troller.
>
> ```
> nand device orion 0xd8000000
> ```

> These controllers don't define any specialized commands. At this writing, their drivers
> don't include write_page or read_page methods, so nand raw_access won't change
> any behavior.

s3c2410   [NAND Driver]
s3c2412   [NAND Driver]
s3c2440   [NAND Driver]
s3c2443   [NAND Driver]
s3c6400   [NAND Driver]
> These S3C family controllers don't have any special nand device options, and don't
> define any specialized commands. At this writing, their drivers don't include write_
> page or read_page methods, so nand raw_access won't change any behavior.

12.6 mFlash

12.6.1 mFlash Configuration

mflash bank *soc base RST_pin target*   [Config Command]
> Configures a mflash for *soc* host bank at address *base*. The pin number format
> depends on the host GPIO naming convention. Currently, the mflash driver supports
> s3c2440 and pxa270.
>
> Example for s3c2440 mflash where *RST pin* is GPIO B1:
>
> ```
> mflash bank $_FLASHNAME s3c2440 0x10000000 1b 0
> ```
>
> Example for pxa270 mflash where *RST pin* is GPIO 43:
>
> ```
> mflash bank $_FLASHNAME pxa270 0x08000000 43 0
> ```

12.6.2 mFlash commands

`mflash config pll` *frequency*   [Command]

Configure mflash PLL. The *frequency* is the mflash input frequency, in Hz. Issuing this command will erase mflash's whole internal nand and write new pll. After this command, mflash needs power-on-reset for normal operation. If pll was newly configured, storage and boot(optional) info also need to be update.

`mflash config boot`   [Command]

Configure bootable option. If bootable option is set, mflash offer the first 8 sectors (4kB) for boot.

`mflash config storage`   [Command]

Configure storage information. For the normal storage operation, this information must be written.

`mflash dump` *num filename offset size*   [Command]

Dump *size* bytes, starting at *offset* bytes from the beginning of the bank *num*, to the file named *filename*.

`mflash probe`   [Command]

Probe mflash.

`mflash write` *num filename offset*   [Command]

Write the binary file *filename* to mflash bank *num*, starting at *offset* bytes from the beginning of the bank.

13 Flash Programming

OpenOCD implements numerous ways to program the target flash, whether internal or external. Programming can be acheived by either using GDB [Programming using GDB], page 127, or using the cmds given in [Flash Programming Commands], page 70.

To simplify using the flash cmds directly a jimtcl script is available that handles the programming and verify stage. OpenOCD will program/verify/reset the target and optionally shutdown.

The script is executed as follows and by default the following actions will be peformed.

1. 'init' is executed.
2. 'reset init' is called to reset and halt the target, any 'reset init' scripts are executed.
3. `flash write_image` is called to erase and write any flash using the filename given.
4. `verify_image` is called if `verify` parameter is given.
5. `reset run` is called if `reset` parameter is given.
6. OpenOCD is shutdown if `exit` parameter is given.

An example of usage is given below. See [program], page 72.

```
# program and verify using elf/hex/s19. verify and reset
# are optional parameters
openocd -f board/stm32f3discovery.cfg \
-c "program filename.elf verify reset exit"

# binary files need the flash address passing
openocd -f board/stm32f3discovery.cfg \
-c "program filename.bin exit 0x08000000"
```

14 PLD/FPGA Commands

Programmable Logic Devices (PLDs) and the more flexible Field Programmable Gate Arrays (FPGAs) are both types of programmable hardware. OpenOCD can support programming them. Although PLDs are generally restrictive (cells are less functional, and there are no special purpose cells for memory or computational tasks), they share the same OpenOCD infrastructure. Accordingly, both are called PLDs here.

14.1 PLD/FPGA Configuration and Commands

As it does for JTAG TAPs, debug targets, and flash chips (both NOR and NAND), OpenOCD maintains a list of PLDs available for use in various commands. Also, each such PLD requires a driver.

They are referenced by the number shown by the `pld devices` command, and new PLDs are defined by `pld device driver_name`.

`pld device` *driver_name tap_name* [*driver_options*]   [Config Command]
> Defines a new PLD device, supported by driver *driver_name*, using the TAP named *tap_name*. The driver may make use of any *driver_options* to configure its behavior.

`pld devices`   [Command]
> Lists the PLDs and their numbers.

`pld load` *num filename*   [Command]
> Loads the file `filename` into the PLD identified by *num*. The file format must be inferred by the driver.

14.2 PLD/FPGA Drivers, Options, and Commands

Drivers may support PLD-specific options to the `pld device` definition command, and may also define commands usable only with that particular type of PLD.

`virtex2` [*no_jstart*]   [FPGA Driver]
> Virtex-II is a family of FPGAs sold by Xilinx. It supports the IEEE 1532 standard for In-System Configuration (ISC).
>
> If *no_jstart* is non-zero, the JSTART instruction is not used after loading the bitstream. While required for Series2, Series3, and Series6, it breaks bitstream loading on Series7.

> `virtex2 read_stat` *num*   [Command]
>> Reads and displays the Virtex-II status register (STAT) for FPGA *num*.

15 General Commands

The commands documented in this chapter here are common commands that you, as a human, may want to type and see the output of. Configuration type commands are documented elsewhere.

Intent:

- **Source Of Commands**
  OpenOCD commands can occur in a configuration script (discussed elsewhere) or typed manually by a human or supplied programatically, or via one of several TCP/IP Ports.

- **From the human**
  A human should interact with the telnet interface (default port: 4444) or via GDB (default port 3333).

  To issue commands from within a GDB session, use the `monitor` command, e.g. use `monitor poll` to issue the `poll` command. All output is relayed through the GDB session.

- **Machine Interface** The Tcl interface's intent is to be a machine interface. The default Tcl port is 5555.

15.1 Daemon Commands

`exit`   [Command]
> Exits the current telnet session.

`help` [*string*]   [Command]
> With no parameters, prints help text for all commands. Otherwise, prints each help-text containing *string*. Not every command provides helptext.
>
> Configuration commands, and commands valid at any time, are explicitly noted in parenthesis. In most cases, no such restriction is listed; this indicates commands which are only available after the configuration stage has completed.

`sleep` *msec* [busy]   [Command]
> Wait for at least *msec* milliseconds before resuming. If `busy` is passed, busy-wait instead of sleeping. (This option is strongly discouraged.) Useful in connection with script files (`script` command and `target_name` configuration).

`shutdown` [error]   [Command]
> Close the OpenOCD daemon, disconnecting all clients (GDB, telnet, other). If option `error` is used, OpenOCD will return a non-zero exit code to the parent process.

`debug_level` [*n*]   [Command]
> Display debug level. If *n* (from 0..3) is provided, then set it to that level. This affects the kind of messages sent to the server log. Level 0 is error messages only; level 1 adds warnings; level 2 adds informational messages; and level 3 adds debugging messages. The default is level 2, but that can be overridden on the command line along with the location of that log file (which is normally the server's standard output). See Chapter 4 [Running], page 12.

`echo` [-*n*] *message*   [Command]

> Logs a message at "user" priority. Output *message* to stdout. Option "-n" suppresses trailing newline.

```
echo "Downloading kernel -- please wait"
```

`log_output` [*filename*]   [Command]

> Redirect logging to *filename*; the initial log output channel is stderr.

`add_script_search_dir` [*directory*]   [Command]

> Add *directory* to the file/script search path.

15.2 Target State handling

In this section "target" refers to a CPU configured as shown earlier (see Chapter 11 [CPU Configuration], page 61). These commands, like many, implicitly refer to a current target which is used to perform the various operations. The current target may be changed by using `targets` command with the name of the target which should become current.

`reg` [(*number*|*name*) [(*value*| 'force')]]   [Command]

> Access a single register by *number* or by its *name*. The target must generally be halted before access to CPU core registers is allowed. Depending on the hardware, some other registers may be accessible while the target is running.
>
> *With no arguments*: list all available registers for the current target, showing number, name, size, value, and cache status. For valid entries, a value is shown; valid entries which are also dirty (and will be written back later) are flagged as such.
>
> *With number/name*: display that register's value. Use *force* argument to read directly from the target, bypassing any internal cache.
>
> *With both number/name and value*: set register's value. Writes may be held in a writeback cache internal to OpenOCD, so that setting the value marks the register as dirty instead of immediately flushing that value. Resuming CPU execution (including by single stepping) or otherwise activating the relevant module will flush such values.
>
> Cores may have surprisingly many registers in their Debug and trace infrastructure:
>
> ```
> > reg
> ===== ARM registers
> (0) r0 (/32): 0x0000D3C2 (dirty)
> (1) r1 (/32): 0xFD61F31C
> (2) r2 (/32)
> ...
> (164) ETM_contextid_comparator_mask (/32)
> >
> ```

`halt` [*ms*]   [Command]
`wait_halt` [*ms*]   [Command]

> The `halt` command first sends a halt request to the target, which `wait_halt` doesn't. Otherwise these behave the same: wait up to *ms* milliseconds, or 5 seconds if there is no parameter, for the target to halt (and enter debug mode). Using 0 as the *ms* parameter prevents OpenOCD from waiting.

Warning: On ARM cores, software using the *wait for interrupt* operation often blocks the JTAG access needed by a `halt` command. This is because that operation also puts the core into a low power mode by gating the core clock; but the core clock is needed to detect JTAG clock transitions.

One partial workaround uses adaptive clocking: when the core is interrupted the operation completes, then JTAG clocks are accepted at least until the interrupt handler completes. However, this workaround is often unusable since the processor, board, and JTAG adapter must all support adaptive JTAG clocking. Also, it can't work until an interrupt is issued.

A more complete workaround is to not use that operation while you work with a JTAG debugger. Tasking environments generaly have idle loops where the body is the *wait for interrupt* operation. (On older cores, it is a coprocessor action; newer cores have a `wfi` instruction.) Such loops can just remove that operation, at the cost of higher power consumption (because the CPU is needlessly clocked).

`resume` [*address*]   [Command]
    Resume the target at its current code position, or the optional *address* if it is provided. OpenOCD will wait 5 seconds for the target to resume.

`step` [*address*]   [Command]
    Single-step the target at its current code position, or the optional *address* if it is provided.

`reset`   [Command]
`reset run`   [Command]
`reset halt`   [Command]
`reset init`   [Command]
    Perform as hard a reset as possible, using SRST if possible. *All defined targets will be reset, and target events will fire during the reset sequence.*

    The optional parameter specifies what should happen after the reset. If there is no parameter, a `reset run` is executed. The other options will not work on all systems. See Chapter 9 [Reset Configuration], page 50.

    — **run** Let the target run

    — **halt** Immediately halt the target

    — **init** Immediately halt the target, and execute the reset-init script

`soft_reset_halt`   [Command]
    Requesting target halt and executing a soft reset. This is often used when a target cannot be reset and halted. The target, after reset is released begins to execute code. OpenOCD attempts to stop the CPU and then sets the program counter back to the reset vector. Unfortunately the code that was executed may have left the hardware in an unknown state.

15.3 I/O Utilities

These commands are available when OpenOCD is built with **--enable-ioutil**. They are mainly useful on embedded targets, notably the ZY1000. Hosts with operating systems have complementary tools.

Note: there are several more such commands.

append_file *filename* [*string*] *   [Command]
> Appends the *string* parameters to the text file **filename**. Each string except the last one is followed by one space. The last string is followed by a newline.

cat *filename*   [Command]
> Reads and displays the text file **filename**.

cp *src_filename dest_filename*   [Command]
> Copies contents from the file **src_filename** into **dest_filename**.

ip   [Command]
> *No description provided.*

ls   [Command]
> *No description provided.*

mac   [Command]
> *No description provided.*

meminfo   [Command]
> Display available RAM memory on OpenOCD host. Used in OpenOCD regression testing scripts.

peek   [Command]
> *No description provided.*

poke   [Command]
> *No description provided.*

rm *filename*   [Command]
> Unlinks the file **filename**.

trunc *filename*   [Command]
> Removes all data in the file **filename**.

15.4 Memory access commands

These commands allow accesses of a specific size to the memory system. Often these are used to configure the current target in some special way. For example - one may need to write certain values to the SDRAM controller to enable SDRAM.

1. Use the **targets** (plural) command to change the current target.
2. In system level scripts these commands are deprecated. Please use their TARGET object siblings to avoid making assumptions about what TAP is the current target, or about MMU configuration.

mdw [*phys*] *addr* [*count*]   [Command]
mdh [*phys*] *addr* [*count*]   [Command]
mdb [*phys*] *addr* [*count*]   [Command]
> Display contents of address *addr*, as 32-bit words (`mdw`), 16-bit halfwords (`mdh`), or 8-bit bytes (`mdb`). When the current target has an MMU which is present and active, *addr* is interpreted as a virtual address. Otherwise, or if the optional *phys* flag is specified, *addr* is interpreted as a physical address. If *count* is specified, displays that many units. (If you want to manipulate the data instead of displaying it, see the `mem2array` primitives.)

mww [*phys*] *addr word*   [Command]
mwh [*phys*] *addr halfword*   [Command]
mwb [*phys*] *addr byte*   [Command]
> Writes the specified *word* (32 bits), *halfword* (16 bits), or *byte* (8-bit) value, at the specified address *addr*. When the current target has an MMU which is present and active, *addr* is interpreted as a virtual address. Otherwise, or if the optional *phys* flag is specified, *addr* is interpreted as a physical address.

15.5 Image loading commands

dump_image *filename address size*   [Command]
> Dump *size* bytes of target memory starting at *address* to the binary file named *filename*.

fast_load   [Command]
> Loads an image stored in memory by `fast_load_image` to the current target. Must be preceeded by fast_load_image.

fast_load_image *filename address* [bin|ihex|elf|s19]   [Command]
> Normally you should be using `load_image` or GDB load. However, for testing purposes or when I/O overhead is significant(OpenOCD running on an embedded host), storing the image in memory and uploading the image to the target can be a way to upload e.g. multiple debug sessions when the binary does not change. Arguments are the same as `load_image`, but the image is stored in OpenOCD host memory, i.e. does not affect target. This approach is also useful when profiling target programming performance as I/O and target programming can easily be profiled separately.

load_image *filename address* [[bin|ihex|elf|s19] min_addr   [Command]
    max_length]
> Load image from file *filename* to target memory offset by *address* from its load address. The file format may optionally be specified (bin, ihex, elf, or s19). In addition the following arguments may be specifed: *min_addr* - ignore data below *min_addr* (this is w.r.t. to the target's load address + *address*) *max_length* - maximum number of bytes to load.

```
proc load_image_bin {fname foffset address length } {
    # Load data from fname filename at foffset offset to
    # target at address. Load at most length bytes.
    load_image $fname [expr $address - $foffset] bin \
```

```
                    $address $length
      }
```

test_image *filename* [*address* [bin|ihex|elf]]   [Command]
> Displays image section sizes and addresses as if *filename* were loaded into target memory starting at *address* (defaults to zero). The file format may optionally be specified (bin, ihex, or elf)

verify_image *filename address* [bin|ihex|elf]   [Command]
> Verify *filename* against target memory starting at *address*. The file format may optionally be specified (bin, ihex, or elf) This will first attempt a comparison using a CRC checksum, if this fails it will try a binary compare.

15.6 Breakpoint and Watchpoint commands

CPUs often make debug modules accessible through JTAG, with hardware support for a handful of code breakpoints and data watchpoints. In addition, CPUs almost always support software breakpoints.

bp [*address len* [hw]]   [Command]
> With no parameters, lists all active breakpoints. Else sets a breakpoint on code execution starting at *address* for *length* bytes. This is a software breakpoint, unless hw is specified in which case it will be a hardware breakpoint.
>
> (See [arm9 vector_catch], page 108, or see [xscale vector_catch], page 112, for similar mechanisms that do not consume hardware breakpoints.)

rbp *address*   [Command]
> Remove the breakpoint at *address*.

rwp *address*   [Command]
> Remove data watchpoint on *address*

wp [*address len* [(r|w|a) [*value* [*mask*]]]]   [Command]
> With no parameters, lists all active watchpoints. Else sets a data watchpoint on data from *address* for *length* bytes. The watch point is an "access" watchpoint unless the r or w parameter is provided, defining it as respectively a read or write watchpoint. If a *value* is provided, that value is used when determining if the watchpoint should trigger. The value may be first be masked using *mask* to mark "don't care" fields.

15.7 Misc Commands

profile *seconds filename* [*start end*]   [Command]
> Profiling samples the CPU's program counter as quickly as possible, which is useful for non-intrusive stochastic profiling. Saves up to 10000 samples in **filename** using "gmon.out" format. Optional **start** and **end** parameters allow to limit the address range.

version   [Command]
> Displays a string identifying the version of this OpenOCD server.

virt2phys *virtual_address*   [Command]
    Requests the current target to map the specified *virtual_address* to its corresponding physical address, and displays the result.

16 Architecture and Core Commands

Most CPUs have specialized JTAG operations to support debugging. OpenOCD packages most such operations in its standard command framework. Some of those operations don't fit well in that framework, so they are exposed here as architecture or implementation (core) specific commands.

16.1 ARM Hardware Tracing

CPUs based on ARM cores may include standard tracing interfaces, based on an "Embedded Trace Module" (ETM) which sends voluminous address and data bus trace records to a "Trace Port".

- Development-oriented boards will sometimes provide a high speed trace connector for collecting that data, when the particular CPU supports such an interface. (The standard connector is a 38-pin Mictor, with both JTAG and trace port support.) Those trace connectors are supported by higher end JTAG adapters and some logic analyzer modules; frequently those modules can buffer several megabytes of trace data. Configuring an ETM coupled to such an external trace port belongs in the board-specific configuration file.

- If the CPU doesn't provide an external interface, it probably has an "Embedded Trace Buffer" (ETB) on the chip, which is a dedicated SRAM. 4KBytes is one common ETB size. Configuring an ETM coupled only to an ETB belongs in the CPU-specific (target) configuration file, since it works the same on all boards.

ETM support in OpenOCD doesn't seem to be widely used yet.

> **Issues:** ETM support may be buggy, and at least some `etm config` parameters should be detected by asking the ETM for them.
>
> ETM trigger events could also implement a kind of complex hardware breakpoint, much more powerful than the simple watchpoint hardware exported by EmbeddedICE modules. *Such breakpoints can be triggered even when using the dummy trace port driver.*
>
> It seems like a GDB hookup should be possible, as well as tracing only during specific states (perhaps *handling IRQ 23* or *calls foo()*).
>
> There should be GUI tools to manipulate saved trace data and help analyse it in conjunction with the source code. It's unclear how much of a common interface is shared with the current XScale trace support, or should be shared with eventual Nexus-style trace module support.
>
> At this writing (November 2009) only ARM7, ARM9, and ARM11 support for ETM modules is available. The code should be able to work with some newer cores; but not all of them support this original style of JTAG access.

16.1.1 ETM Configuration

ETM setup is coupled with the trace port driver configuration.

`etm config` *target width mode clocking driver*   [Config Command]
> Declares the ETM associated with *target*, and associates it with a given trace port driver. See [Trace Port Drivers], page 105.

Several of the parameters must reflect the trace port capabilities, which are a function of silicon capabilties (exposed later using `etm info`) and of what hardware is connected to that port (such as an external pod, or ETB). The *width* must be either 4, 8, or 16, except with ETMv3.0 and newer modules which may also support 1, 2, 24, 32, 48, and 64 bit widths. (With those versions, `etm info` also shows whether the selected port width and mode are supported.)

The *mode* must be `normal`, `multiplexed`, or `demultiplexed`. The *clocking* must be `half` or `full`.

> **Warning:** With ETMv3.0 and newer, the bits set with the *mode* and *clocking* parameters both control the mode. This modified mode does not map to the values supported by previous ETM modules, so this syntax is subject to change.

> **Note:** You can see the ETM registers using the `reg` command. Not all possible registers are present in every ETM. Most of the registers are write-only, and are used to configure what CPU activities are traced.

etm info   [Command]
Displays information about the current target's ETM. This includes resource counts from the `ETM_CONFIG` register, as well as silicon capabilities (except on rather old modules). from the `ETM_SYS_CONFIG` register.

etm status   [Command]
Displays status of the current target's ETM and trace port driver: is the ETM idle, or is it collecting data? Did trace data overflow? Was it triggered?

etm tracemode [*type context_id_bits cycle_accurate branch_output*]   [Command]
Displays what data that ETM will collect. If arguments are provided, first configures that data. When the configuration changes, tracing is stopped and any buffered trace data is invalidated.

- *type* ... describing how data accesses are traced, when they pass any ViewData filtering that that was set up. The value is one of `none` (save nothing), `data` (save data), `address` (save addresses), `all` (save data and addresses)

- *context_id_bits* ... 0, 8, 16, or 32

- *cycle_accurate* ... `enable` or `disable` cycle-accurate instruction tracing. Before ETMv3, enabling this causes much extra data to be recorded.

- *branch_output* ... `enable` or `disable`. Disable this unless you need to try reconstructing the instruction trace stream without an image of the code.

etm trigger_debug (enable|disable)   [Command]
Displays whether ETM triggering debug entry (like a breakpoint) is enabled or disabled, after optionally modifying that configuration. The default behaviour is `disable`. Any change takes effect after the next `etm start`.

By using script commands to configure ETM registers, you can make the processor enter debug state automatically when certain conditions, more complex than supported by the breakpoint hardware, happen.

16.1.2 ETM Trace Operation

After setting up the ETM, you can use it to collect data. That data can be exported to files for later analysis. It can also be parsed with OpenOCD, for basic sanity checking.

To configure what is being traced, you will need to write various trace registers using `reg` ETM_* commands. For the definitions of these registers, read ARM publication *IHI 0014, "Embedded Trace Macrocell, Architecture Specification"*. Be aware that most of the relevant registers are write-only, and that ETM resources are limited. There are only a handful of address comparators, data comparators, counters, and so on.

Examples of scenarios you might arrange to trace include:

- Code flow within a function, *excluding* subroutines it calls. Use address range comparators to enable tracing for instruction access within that function's body.

- Code flow within a function, *including* subroutines it calls. Use the sequencer and address comparators to activate tracing on an "entered function" state, then deactivate it by exiting that state when the function's exit code is invoked.

- Code flow starting at the fifth invocation of a function, combining one of the above models with a counter.

- CPU data accesses to the registers for a particular device, using address range comparators and the ViewData logic.

- Such data accesses only during IRQ handling, combining the above model with sequencer triggers which on entry and exit to the IRQ handler.

- *... more*

At this writing, September 2009, there are no Tcl utility procedures to help set up any common tracing scenarios.

etm analyze   [Command]
    Reads trace data into memory, if it wasn't already present. Decodes and prints the data that was collected.

etm dump *filename*   [Command]
    Stores the captured trace data in `filename`.

etm image *filename* [*base_address*] [*type*]   [Command]
    Opens an image file.

etm load *filename*   [Command]
    Loads captured trace data from `filename`.

etm start   [Command]
    Starts trace data collection.

etm stop   [Command]
    Stops trace data collection.

16.1.3 Trace Port Drivers

To use an ETM trace port it must be associated with a driver.

dummy   [Trace Port Driver]

> Use the **dummy** driver if you are configuring an ETM that's not connected to anything (on-chip ETB or off-chip trace connector). *This driver lets OpenOCD talk to the ETM, but it does not expose any trace data collection.*
>
> **etm_dummy config** *target*   [Config Command]
>> Associates the ETM for *target* with a dummy driver.

etb   [Trace Port Driver]

> Use the **etb** driver if you are configuring an ETM to use on-chip ETB memory.
>
> **etb config** *target etb_tap*   [Config Command]
>> Associates the ETM for *target* with the ETB at *etb_tap*. You can see the ETB registers using the **reg** command.
>
> **etb trigger_percent** [*percent*]   [Command]
>> This displays, or optionally changes, ETB behavior after the ETM's configured *trigger* event fires. It controls how much more trace data is saved after the (single) trace trigger becomes active.
>>
>> - The default corresponds to *trace around* usage, recording 50 percent data before the event and the rest afterwards.
>> - The minimum value of *percent* is 2 percent, recording almost exclusively data before the trigger. Such extreme *trace before* usage can help figure out what caused that event to happen.
>> - The maximum value of *percent* is 100 percent, recording data almost exclusively after the event. This extreme *trace after* usage might help sort out how the event caused trouble.

oocd_trace   [Trace Port Driver]

> This driver isn't available unless OpenOCD was explicitly configured with the --enable-oocd_trace option. You probably don't want to configure it unless you've built the appropriate prototype hardware; it's *proof-of-concept* software.
>
> Use the **oocd_trace** driver if you are configuring an ETM that's connected to an off-chip trace connector.
>
> **oocd_trace config** *target tty*   [Config Command]
>> Associates the ETM for *target* with a trace driver which collects data through the serial port *tty*.
>
> **oocd_trace resync**   [Command]
>> Re-synchronizes with the capture clock.
>
> **oocd_trace status**   [Command]
>> Reports whether the capture clock is locked or not.

16.2 Generic ARM

These commands should be available on all ARM processors. They are available in addition to other core-specific commands that may be available.

arm core_state [arm|thumb] [Command]

Displays the core_state, optionally changing it to process either **arm** or **thumb** instructions. The target may later be resumed in the currently set core_state. (Processors may also support the Jazelle state, but that is not currently supported in OpenOCD.)

arm disassemble *address* [*count* [**thumb**]] [Command]

Disassembles *count* instructions starting at *address*. If *count* is not specified, a single instruction is disassembled. If **thumb** is specified, or the low bit of the address is set, Thumb2 (mixed 16/32-bit) instructions are used; else ARM (32-bit) instructions are used. (Processors may also support the Jazelle state, but those instructions are not currently understood by OpenOCD.)

Note that all Thumb instructions are Thumb2 instructions, so older processors (without Thumb2 support) will still see correct disassembly of Thumb code. Also, ThumbEE opcodes are the same as Thumb2, with a handful of exceptions. ThumbEE disassembly currently has no explicit support.

arm mcr *pX op1 CRn CRm op2 value* [Command]

Write *value* to a coprocessor *pX* register passing parameters *CRn*, *CRm*, opcodes *opc1* and *opc2*, and using the MCR instruction. (Parameter sequence matches the ARM instruction, but omits an ARM register.)

arm mrc *pX coproc op1 CRn CRm op2* [Command]

Read a coprocessor *pX* register passing parameters *CRn*, *CRm*, opcodes *opc1* and *opc2*, and the MRC instruction. Returns the result so it can be manipulated by Jim scripts. (Parameter sequence matches the ARM instruction, but omits an ARM register.)

arm reg [Command]

Display a table of all banked core registers, fetching the current value from every core mode if necessary.

arm semihosting [enable|disable] [Command]

Display status of semihosting, after optionally changing that status.

Semihosting allows for code executing on an ARM target to use the I/O facilities on the host computer i.e. the system where OpenOCD is running. The target application must be linked against a library implementing the ARM semihosting convention that forwards operation requests by using a special SVC instruction that is trapped at the Supervisor Call vector by OpenOCD.

16.3 ARMv4 and ARMv5 Architecture

The ARMv4 and ARMv5 architectures are widely used in embedded systems, and introduced core parts of the instruction set in use today. That includes the Thumb instruction set, introduced in the ARMv4T variant.

16.3.1 ARM7 and ARM9 specific commands

These commands are specific to ARM7 and ARM9 cores, like ARM7TDMI, ARM720T, ARM9TDMI, ARM920T or ARM926EJ-S. They are available in addition to the ARM commands, and any other core-specific commands that may be available.

arm7_9 dbgrq [enable|disable]   [Command]

> Displays the value of the flag controlling use of the the EmbeddedIce DBGRQ signal to force entry into debug mode, instead of breakpoints. If a boolean parameter is provided, first assigns that flag.

> This should be safe for all but ARM7TDMI-S cores (like NXP LPC). This feature is enabled by default on most ARM9 cores, including ARM9TDMI, ARM920T, and ARM926EJ-S.

arm7_9 dcc_downloads [enable|disable]   [Command]

> Displays the value of the flag controlling use of the debug communications channel (DCC) to write larger (>128 byte) amounts of memory. If a boolean parameter is provided, first assigns that flag.

> DCC downloads offer a huge speed increase, but might be unsafe, especially with targets running at very low speeds. This command was introduced with OpenOCD rev. 60, and requires a few bytes of working area.

arm7_9 fast_memory_access [enable|disable]   [Command]

> Displays the value of the flag controlling use of memory writes and reads that don't check completion of the operation. If a boolean parameter is provided, first assigns that flag.

> This provides a huge speed increase, especially with USB JTAG cables (FT2232), but might be unsafe if used with targets running at very low speeds, like the 32kHz startup clock of an AT91RM9200.

16.3.2 ARM720T specific commands

These commands are available to ARM720T based CPUs, which are implementations of the ARMv4T architecture based on the ARM7TDMI-S integer core. They are available in addition to the ARM and ARM7/ARM9 commands.

arm720t cp15 *opcode* [*value*]   [Command]

> *DEPRECATED – avoid using this. Use the* **arm mrc** *or* **arm mcr** *commands instead.*

> Display cp15 register returned by the ARM instruction *opcode*; else if a *value* is provided, that value is written to that register. The *opcode* should be the value of either an MRC or MCR instruction.

16.3.3 ARM9 specific commands

ARM9-family cores are built around ARM9TDMI or ARM9E (including ARM9EJS) integer processors. Such cores include the ARM920T, ARM926EJ-S, and ARM966.

arm9 vector_catch [all|none|*list***]**   [Command]

> Vector Catch hardware provides a sort of dedicated breakpoint for hardware events such as reset, interrupt, and abort. You can use this to conserve normal breakpoint

resources, so long as you're not concerned with code that branches directly to those hardware vectors.

This always finishes by listing the current configuration. If parameters are provided, it first reconfigures the vector catch hardware to intercept **all** of the hardware vectors, **none** of them, or a list with one or more of the following: **reset undef swi pabt dabt irq fiq**.

16.3.4 ARM920T specific commands

These commands are available to ARM920T based CPUs, which are implementations of the ARMv4T architecture built using the ARM9TDMI integer core. They are available in addition to the ARM, ARM7/ARM9, and ARM9 commands.

arm920t cache_info   [Command]
> Print information about the caches found. This allows to see whether your target is an ARM920T (2x16kByte cache) or ARM922T (2x8kByte cache).

arm920t cp15 *regnum* [*value*]   [Command]
> Display cp15 register *regnum*; else if a *value* is provided, that value is written to that register. This uses "physical access" and the register number is as shown in bits 38..33 of table 9-9 in the ARM920T TRM. (Not all registers can be written.)

arm920t cp15i *opcode* [*value* [*address*]]   [Command]
> *DEPRECATED – avoid using this. Use the* **arm mrc** *or* **arm mcr** *commands instead.*
>
> Interpreted access using ARM instruction *opcode*, which should be the value of either an MRC or MCR instruction (as shown tables 9-11, 9-12, and 9-13 in the ARM920T TRM). If no *value* is provided, the result is displayed. Else if that value is written using the specified *address*, or using zero if no other address is provided.

arm920t read_cache *filename*   [Command]
> Dump the content of ICache and DCache to a file named **filename**.

arm920t read_mmu *filename*   [Command]
> Dump the content of the ITLB and DTLB to a file named **filename**.

16.3.5 ARM926ej-s specific commands

These commands are available to ARM926ej-s based CPUs, which are implementations of the ARMv5TEJ architecture based on the ARM9EJ-S integer core. They are available in addition to the ARM, ARM7/ARM9, and ARM9 commands.

The Feroceon cores also support these commands, although they are not built from ARM926ej-s designs.

arm926ejs cache_info   [Command]
> Print information about the caches found.

16.3.6 ARM966E specific commands

These commands are available to ARM966 based CPUs, which are implementations of the ARMv5TE architecture. They are available in addition to the ARM, ARM7/ARM9, and ARM9 commands.

arm966e cp15 *regnum* [*value*]   [Command]

    Display cp15 register *regnum*; else if a *value* is provided, that value is written to that register. The six bit *regnum* values are bits 37..32 from table 7-2 of the ARM966E-S TRM. There is no current control over bits 31..30 from that table, as required for BIST support.

16.3.7 XScale specific commands

Some notes about the debug implementation on the XScale CPUs:

The XScale CPU provides a special debug-only mini-instruction cache (mini-IC) in which exception vectors and target-resident debug handler code are placed by OpenOCD. In order to get access to the CPU, OpenOCD must point vector 0 (the reset vector) to the entry of the debug handler. However, this means that the complete first cacheline in the mini-IC is marked valid, which makes the CPU fetch all exception handlers from the mini-IC, ignoring the code in RAM.

To address this situation, OpenOCD provides the **xscale vector_table** command, which allows the user to explicity write individual entries to either the high or low vector table stored in the mini-IC.

It is recommended to place a pc-relative indirect branch in the vector table, and put the branch destination somewhere in memory. Doing so makes sure the code in the vector table stays constant regardless of code layout in memory:

```
_vectors:
        ldr      pc,[pc,#0x100-8]
        ldr      pc,[pc,#0x100-8]
        ldr      pc,[pc,#0x100-8]
        ldr      pc,[pc,#0x100-8]
        ldr      pc,[pc,#0x100-8]
        ldr      pc,[pc,#0x100-8]
        ldr      pc,[pc,#0x100-8]
        ldr      pc,[pc,#0x100-8]
        .org 0x100
        .long real_reset_vector
        .long real_ui_handler
        .long real_swi_handler
        .long real_pf_abort
        .long real_data_abort
        .long 0 /* unused */
        .long real_irq_handler
        .long real_fiq_handler
```

Alternatively, you may choose to keep some or all of the mini-IC vector table entries synced with those written to memory by your system software. The mini-IC can not be modified while the processor is executing, but for each vector table entry not previously defined using the **xscale vector_table** command, OpenOCD will copy the value from memory to the mini-IC every time execution resumes from a halt. This is done for both high and low vector tables (although the table not in use may not be mapped to valid memory, and in this case that copy operation will silently fail). This means that you will need to briefly halt execution at some strategic point during system start-up; e.g., after the software has initialized the vector table, but before exceptions are enabled. A breakpoint can be used to accomplish this once the appropriate location in the start-up code has been identified. A watchpoint over the vector table region is helpful in finding the location if you're not sure. Note that the same situation exists any time the vector table is modified by the system software.

The debug handler must be placed somewhere in the address space using the **xscale debug_handler** command. The allowed locations for the debug handler are either (0x800 - 0x1fef800) or (0xfe000800 - 0xfffff800). The default value is 0xfe000800.

XScale has resources to support two hardware breakpoints and two watchpoints. However, the following restrictions on watchpoint functionality apply: (1) the value and mask arguments to the **wp** command are not supported, (2) the watchpoint length must be a power of two and not less than four, and can not be greater than the watchpoint address, and (3) a watchpoint with a length greater than four consumes all the watchpoint hardware resources. This means that at any one time, you can have enabled either two watchpoints with a length of four, or one watchpoint with a length greater than four.

These commands are available to XScale based CPUs, which are implementations of the ARMv5TE architecture.

xscale analyze_trace   [Command]
    Displays the contents of the trace buffer.

xscale cache_clean_address *address*   [Command]
    Changes the address used when cleaning the data cache.

xscale cache_info   [Command]
    Displays information about the CPU caches.

xscale cp15 *regnum* [*value*]   [Command]
    Display cp15 register *regnum*; else if a *value* is provided, that value is written to that register.

xscale debug_handler *target address*   [Command]
    Changes the address used for the specified target's debug handler.

xscale dcache [enable|disable]   [Command]
    Enables or disable the CPU's data cache.

xscale dump_trace *filename*   [Command]
    Dumps the raw contents of the trace buffer to **filename**.

xscale icache [enable|disable]   [Command]
    Enables or disable the CPU's instruction cache.

xscale mmu [enable|disable]   [Command]
    Enables or disable the CPU's memory management unit.

xscale trace_buffer [enable|disable [fill [*n*] | wrap]]   [Command]
    Displays the trace buffer status, after optionally enabling or disabling the trace buffer and modifying how it is emptied.

xscale trace_image *filename* [*offset* [*type*]]   [Command]
> Opens a trace image from `filename`, optionally rebasing its segment addresses by *offset*. The image *type* may be one of `bin` (binary), `ihex` (Intel hex), `elf` (ELF file), `s19` (Motorola s19), `mem`, or `builder`.

xscale vector_catch [*mask*]   [Command]
> Display a bitmask showing the hardware vectors to catch. If the optional parameter is provided, first set the bitmask to that value.
>
> The mask bits correspond with bit 16..23 in the DCSR:

> | | |
> |---|---|
> | 0x01 | Trap Reset |
> | 0x02 | Trap Undefined Instructions |
> | 0x04 | Trap Software Interrupt |
> | 0x08 | Trap Prefetch Abort |
> | 0x10 | Trap Data Abort |
> | 0x20 | reserved |
> | 0x40 | Trap IRQ |
> | 0x80 | Trap FIQ |

xscale vector_table [(low|high) *index value*]   [Command]
> Set an entry in the mini-IC vector table. There are two tables: one for low vectors (at 0x00000000), and one for high vectors (0xFFFF0000), each holding the 8 exception vectors. *index* can be 1-7, because vector 0 points to the debug handler entry and can not be overwritten. *value* holds the 32-bit opcode that is placed in the mini-IC.
>
> Without arguments, the current settings are displayed.

16.4 ARMv6 Architecture

16.4.1 ARM11 specific commands

arm11 memwrite burst [enable|disable]   [Command]
> Displays the value of the memwrite burst-enable flag, which is enabled by default. If a boolean parameter is provided, first assigns that flag. Burst writes are only used for memory writes larger than 1 word. They improve performance by assuming that the CPU has read each data word over JTAG and completed its write before the next word arrives, instead of polling for a status flag to verify that completion. This is usually safe, because JTAG runs much slower than the CPU.

arm11 memwrite error_fatal [enable|disable]   [Command]
> Displays the value of the memwrite error_fatal flag, which is enabled by default. If a boolean parameter is provided, first assigns that flag. When set, certain memory write errors cause earlier transfer termination.

arm11 step_irq_enable [enable|disable]   [Command]
> Displays the value of the flag controlling whether IRQs are enabled during single stepping; they are disabled by default. If a boolean parameter is provided, first assigns that.

arm11 vcr [*value*]   [Command]
>   Displays the value of the *Vector Catch Register (VCR)*, coprocessor 14 register 7. If
>   *value* is defined, first assigns that.
>
>   Vector Catch hardware provides dedicated breakpoints for certain hardware events.
>   The specific bit values are core-specific (as in fact is using coprocessor 14 register 7
>   itself) but all current ARM11 cores *except the ARM1176* use the same six bits.

16.5 ARMv7 Architecture

16.5.1 ARMv7 Debug Access Port (DAP) specific commands

These commands are specific to ARM architecture v7 Debug Access Port (DAP), included
on Cortex-M and Cortex-A systems. They are available in addition to other core-specific
commands that may be available.

dap apid [*num*]   [Command]
>   Displays ID register from AP *num*, defaulting to the currently selected AP.

dap apsel [*num*]   [Command]
>   Select AP *num*, defaulting to 0.

dap baseaddr [*num*]   [Command]
>   Displays debug base address from MEM-AP *num*, defaulting to the currently selected
>   AP.

dap info [*num*]   [Command]
>   Displays the ROM table for MEM-AP *num*, defaulting to the currently selected AP.

dap memaccess [*value*]   [Command]
>   Displays the number of extra tck cycles in the JTAG idle to use for MEM-AP memory
>   bus access [0-255], giving additional time to respond to reads. If *value* is defined, first
>   assigns that.

dap apcsw [*0 / 1*]   [Command]
>   fix CSW_SPROT from register AP_REG_CSW on selected dap. Defaulting to 0.

16.5.2 ARMv7-M specific commands

tpiu config (disable | ((external | internal (*filename*** | -))**   [Command]
>   **(sync *port_width* | ((manchester | uart) *formatter_enable*))**
>   ***TRACECLKIN_freq* [*trace_freq*]))**
>   ARMv7-M architecture provides several modules to generate debugging information
>   internally (ITM, DWT and ETM). Their output is directed through TPIU to be
>   captured externally either on an SWO pin (this configuration is called SWV) or on a
>   synchronous parallel trace port.
>
>   This command configures the TPIU module of the target and, if internal capture mode
>   is selected, starts to capture trace output by using the debugger adapter features.
>
>   Some targets require additional actions to be performed in the **trace-config** handler
>   for trace port to be activated.
>
>   Command options:

  − **disable** disable TPIU handling;
  − **external** configure TPIU to let user capture trace output externally (with an additional UART or logic analyzer hardware);
  − **internal** *filename* configure TPIU and debug adapter to gather trace data and append it to *filename* (which can be either a regular file or a named pipe);
  − **internal** – configure TPIU and debug adapter to gather trace data, but not write to any file. Useful in conjunction with the **tcl_trace** command;
  − **sync** *port_width* use synchronous parallel trace output mode, and set port width to *port_width*;
  − **manchester** use asynchronous SWO mode with Manchester coding;
  − **uart** use asynchronous SWO mode with NRZ (same as regular UART 8N1) coding;
  − *formatter_enable* is **on** or **off** to enable or disable TPIU formatter which needs to be used when both ITM and ETM data is to be output via SWO;
  − *TRACECLKIN_freq* this should be specified to match target's current TRACE-CLKIN frequency (usually the same as HCLK);
  − *trace_freq* trace port frequency. Can be omitted in internal mode to let the adapter driver select the maximum supported rate automatically.

Example usage:
  1. STM32L152 board is programmed with an application that configures PLL to provide core clock with 24MHz frequency; to use ITM output it's enough to:

```
#include <libopencm3/cm3/itm.h>
  ...
 ITM_STIM8(0) = c;
  ...
```

  (the most obvious way is to use the first stimulus port for printf, for that this ITM_STIM8 assignment can be used inside _write(); to make it blocking to avoid data loss, add **while (!(ITM_STIM8(0) & ITM_STIM_FIFOREADY));**);
  2. An FT2232H UART is connected to the SWO pin of the board;
  3. Commands to configure UART for 12MHz baud rate:

```
$ setserial /dev/ttyUSB1 spd_cust divisor 5
$ stty -F /dev/ttyUSB1 38400
```

  (FT2232H's base frequency is 60MHz, spd_cust allows to alias 38400 baud with our custom divisor to get 12MHz)
  4. itmdump -f /dev/ttyUSB1 -d1
  5. OpenOCD invocation line:

```
openocd -f interface/stlink-v2-1.cfg \
        -c "transport select hla_swd" \
        -f target/stm32l1.cfg \
        -c "tpiu config external uart off 24000000 12000000"
```

itm port *port* (0|1|on|off)   [Command]
  Enable or disable trace output for ITM stimulus *port* (counting from 0). Port 0 is enabled on target creation automatically.

`itm ports (0|1|on|off)`   [Command]
> Enable or disable trace output for all ITM stimulus ports.

16.5.3 Cortex-M specific commands

`cortex_m maskisr (auto|on|off)`   [Command]
> Control masking (disabling) interrupts during target step/resume.
>
> The `auto` option handles interrupts during stepping a way they get served but don't disturb the program flow. The step command first allows pending interrupt handlers to execute, then disables interrupts and steps over the next instruction where the core was halted. After the step interrupts are enabled again. If the interrupt handlers don't complete within 500ms, the step command leaves with the core running.
>
> Note that a free breakpoint is required for the `auto` option. If no breakpoint is available at the time of the step, then the step is taken with interrupts enabled, i.e. the same way the `off` option does.
>
> Default is `auto`.

`cortex_m vector_catch [all|none|`*list*`]`   [Command]
> Vector Catch hardware provides dedicated breakpoints for certain hardware events.
>
> Parameters request interception of `all` of these hardware event vectors, `none` of them, or one or more of the following: `hard_err` for a HardFault exception; `mm_err` for a MemManage exception; `bus_err` for a BusFault exception; `irq_err`, `state_err`, `chk_err`, or `nocp_err` for various UsageFault exceptions; or `reset`. If NVIC setup code does not enable them, MemManage, BusFault, and UsageFault exceptions are mapped to HardFault. UsageFault checks for divide-by-zero and unaligned access must also be explicitly enabled.
>
> This finishes by listing the current vector catch configuration.

`cortex_m reset_config (srst|sysresetreq|vectreset)`   [Command]
> Control reset handling. The default `srst` is to use srst if fitted, otherwise fallback to `vectreset`.
>
> — `srst` use hardware srst if fitted otherwise fallback to `vectreset`.
> — `sysresetreq` use NVIC SYSRESETREQ to reset system.
> — `vectreset` use NVIC VECTRESET to reset system.
>
> Using `vectreset` is a safe option for all current Cortex-M cores. This however has the disadvantage of only resetting the core, all peripherals are uneffected. A solution would be to use a `reset-init` event handler to manually reset the peripherals. See [Target Events], page 66.

16.6 Intel Architecture

Intel Quark X10xx is the first product in the Quark family of SoCs. It is an IA-32 (Pentium x86 ISA) compatible SoC. The core CPU in the X10xx is codenamed Lakemont. Lakemont version 1 (LMT1) is used in X10xx. The CPU TAP (Lakemont TAP) is used for software debug and the CLTAP is used for SoC level operations. Useful docs are here: https://communities.intel.com/community/makers/documentation

- Intel Quark SoC X1000 OpenOCD/GDB/Eclipse App Note (web search for doc num 330015)
- Intel Quark SoC X1000 Debug Operations User Guide (web search for doc num 329866)
- Intel Quark SoC X1000 Datasheet (web search for doc num 329676)

16.6.1 x86 32-bit specific commands

The three main address spaces for x86 are memory, I/O and configuration space. These commands allow a user to read and write to the 64Kbyte I/O address space.

x86_32 idw *address*   [Command]
> Display the contents of a 32-bit I/O port from address range 0x0000 - 0xffff.

x86_32 idh *address*   [Command]
> Display the contents of a 16-bit I/O port from address range 0x0000 - 0xffff.

x86_32 idb *address*   [Command]
> Display the contents of a 8-bit I/O port from address range 0x0000 - 0xffff.

x86_32 iww *address*   [Command]
> Write the contents of a 32-bit I/O port to address range 0x0000 - 0xffff.

x86_32 iwh *address*   [Command]
> Write the contents of a 16-bit I/O port to address range 0x0000 - 0xffff.

x86_32 iwb *address*   [Command]
> Write the contents of a 8-bit I/O port to address range 0x0000 - 0xffff.

16.7 OpenRISC Architecture

The OpenRISC CPU is a soft core. It is used in a programmable SoC which can be configured with any of the TAP / Debug Unit available.

16.7.1 TAP and Debug Unit selection commands

tap_select (vjtag|mohor|xilinx_bscan)   [Command]
> Select between the Altera Virtual JTAG , Xilinx Virtual JTAG and Mohor TAP.

du_select (adv|mohor) [*option*]   [Command]
> Select between the Advanced Debug Interface and the classic one.
>
> An option can be passed as a second argument to the debug unit.
>
> When using the Advanced Debug Interface, option = 1 means the RTL core is configured with ADBG_USE_HISPEED = 1. This configuration skips status checking between bytes while doing read or write bursts.

16.7.2 Registers commands

addreg [*name*] [*address*] [*feature*] [*reg_group*]   [Command]
> Add a new register in the cpu register list. This register will be included in the generated target descriptor file.

[**feature**] must be "org.gnu.gdb.or1k.group[0..10]".

[**reg_group**] can be anything. The default register list defines "system", "dmmu", "immu", "dcache", "icache", "mac", "debug", "perf", "power", "pic" and "timer" groups.

example:

```
addreg rtest 0x1234 org.gnu.gdb.or1k.group0 system
```

`readgroup (group)`   [Command]

Display all registers in *group*.

group can be "system", "dmmu", "immu", "dcache", "icache", "mac", "debug", "perf", "power", "pic", "timer" or any new group created with addreg command.

16.8 Software Debug Messages and Tracing

OpenOCD can process certain requests from target software, when the target uses appropriate libraries. The most powerful mechanism is semihosting, but there is also a lighter weight mechanism using only the DCC channel.

Currently `target_request debugmsgs` is supported only for `arm7_9` and `cortex_m` cores. These messages are received as part of target polling, so you need to have `poll on` active to receive them. They are intrusive in that they will affect program execution times. If that is a problem, see [ARM Hardware Tracing], page 103.

See `libdcc` in the contrib dir for more details. In addition to sending strings, characters, and arrays of various size integers from the target, `libdcc` also exports a software trace point mechanism. The target being debugged may issue trace messages which include a 24-bit *trace point* number. Trace point support includes two distinct mechanisms, each supported by a command:

- *History* ... A circular buffer of trace points can be set up, and then displayed at any time. This tracks where code has been, which can be invaluable in finding out how some fault was triggered.

  The buffer may overflow, since it collects records continuously. It may be useful to use some of the 24 bits to represent a particular event, and other bits to hold data.

- *Counting* ... An array of counters can be set up, and then displayed at any time. This can help establish code coverage and identify hot spots.

  The array of counters is directly indexed by the trace point number, so trace points with higher numbers are not counted.

Linux-ARM kernels have a "Kernel low-level debugging via EmbeddedICE DCC channel" option (CONFIG_DEBUG_ICEDCC, depends on CONFIG_DEBUG_LL) which uses this mechanism to deliver messages before a serial console can be activated. This is not the same format used by `libdcc`. Other software, such as the U-Boot boot loader, sometimes does the same thing.

`target_request debugmsgs [enable|disable|charmsg]`   [Command]

Displays current handling of target DCC message requests. These messages may be sent to the debugger while the target is running. The optional `enable` and `charmsg` parameters both enable the messages, while `disable` disables them.

With `charmsg` the DCC words each contain one character, as used by Linux with CONFIG_DEBUG_ICEDCC; otherwise the libdcc format is used.

`trace history [clear|`*count*`]`   [Command]
> With no parameter, displays all the trace points that have triggered in the order they triggered. With the parameter `clear`, erases all current trace history records. With a *count* parameter, allocates space for that many history records.

`trace point [clear|`*identifier*`]`   [Command]
> With no parameter, displays all trace point identifiers and how many times they have been triggered. With the parameter `clear`, erases all current trace point counters. With a numeric *identifier* parameter, creates a new a trace point counter and associates it with that identifier.
>
> *Important:* The identifier and the trace point number are not related except by this command. These trace point numbers always start at zero (from server startup, or after `trace point clear`) and count up from there.

17 JTAG Commands

Most general purpose JTAG commands have been presented earlier. (See [JTAG Speed], page 48, Chapter 9 [Reset Configuration], page 50, and Chapter 10 [TAP Declaration], page 55.) Lower level JTAG commands, as presented here, may be needed to work with targets which require special attention during operations such as reset or initialization.

To use these commands you will need to understand some of the basics of JTAG, including:

- A JTAG scan chain consists of a sequence of individual TAP devices such as a CPUs.

- Control operations involve moving each TAP through the same standard state machine (in parallel) using their shared TMS and clock signals.

- Data transfer involves shifting data through the chain of instruction or data registers of each TAP, writing new register values while the reading previous ones.

- Data register sizes are a function of the instruction active in a given TAP, while instruction register sizes are fixed for each TAP. All TAPs support a BYPASS instruction with a single bit data register.

- The way OpenOCD differentiates between TAP devices is by shifting different instructions into (and out of) their instruction registers.

17.1 Low Level JTAG Commands

These commands are used by developers who need to access JTAG instruction or data registers, possibly controlling the order of TAP state transitions. If you're not debugging OpenOCD internals, or bringing up a new JTAG adapter or a new type of TAP device (like a CPU or JTAG router), you probably won't need to use these commands. In a debug session that doesn't use JTAG for its transport protocol, these commands are not available.

drscan *tap* [*numbits value*]+ [**-endstate** *tap_state*]   [Command]
> Loads the data register of *tap* with a series of bit fields that specify the entire register. Each field is *numbits* bits long with a numeric *value* (hexadecimal encouraged). The return value holds the original value of each of those fields.
>
> For example, a 38 bit number might be specified as one field of 32 bits then one of 6 bits. *For portability, never pass fields which are more than 32 bits long. Many OpenOCD implementations do not support 64-bit (or larger) integer values.*
>
> All TAPs other than *tap* must be in BYPASS mode. The single bit in their data registers does not matter.
>
> When *tap_state* is specified, the JTAG state machine is left in that state. For example DRPAUSE might be specified, so that more instructions can be issued before re-entering the RUN/IDLE state. If the end state is not specified, the RUN/IDLE state is entered.
>
> > **Warning:** OpenOCD does not record information about data register lengths, so *it is important that you get the bit field lengths right*. Remember that different JTAG instructions refer to different data registers, which may have different lengths. Moreover, those lengths may not be fixed; the SCAN_N instruction can change the length of the register accessed by the INTEST instruction (by connecting a different scan chain).

`flush_count`   [Command]

Returns the number of times the JTAG queue has been flushed. This may be used for performance tuning.

For example, flushing a queue over USB involves a minimum latency, often several milliseconds, which does not change with the amount of data which is written. You may be able to identify performance problems by finding tasks which waste bandwidth by flushing small transfers too often, instead of batching them into larger operations.

`irscan` [tap instruction]+ [-endstate tap_state]   [Command]

For each tap listed, loads the instruction register with its associated numeric instruction. (The number of bits in that instruction may be displayed using the `scan_chain` command.) For other TAPs, a BYPASS instruction is loaded.

When tap_state is specified, the JTAG state machine is left in that state. For example IRPAUSE might be specified, so the data register can be loaded before re-entering the RUN/IDLE state. If the end state is not specified, the RUN/IDLE state is entered.

> **Note:** OpenOCD currently supports only a single field for instruction register values, unlike data register values. For TAPs where the instruction register length is more than 32 bits, portable scripts currently must issue only BYPASS instructions.

`jtag_reset` trst srst   [Command]

Set values of reset signals. The trst and srst parameter values may be 0, indicating that reset is inactive (pulled or driven high), or 1, indicating it is active (pulled or driven low). The `reset_config` command should already have been used to configure how the board and JTAG adapter treat these two signals, and to say if either signal is even present. See Chapter 9 [Reset Configuration], page 50.

Note that TRST is specially handled. It actually signifies JTAG's RESET state. So if the board doesn't support the optional TRST signal, or it doesn't support it along with the specified SRST value, JTAG reset is triggered with TMS and TCK signals instead of the TRST signal. And no matter how that JTAG reset is triggered, once the scan chain enters RESET with TRST inactive, TAP `post-reset` events are delivered to all TAPs with handlers for that event.

`pathmove` start_state [next_state ...]   [Command]

Start by moving to start_state, which must be one of the stable states. Unless it is the only state given, this will often be the current state, so that no TCK transitions are needed. Then, in a series of single state transitions (conforming to the JTAG state machine) shift to each next_state in sequence, one per TCK cycle. The final state must also be stable.

`runtest` num_cycles   [Command]

Move to the RUN/IDLE state, and execute at least num_cycles of the JTAG clock (TCK). Instructions often need some time to execute before they take effect.

`verify_ircapture` (enable|disable)   [Command]

Verify values captured during IRCAPTURE and returned during IR scans. Default is enabled, but this can be overridden by `verify_jtag`. This flag is ignored when validating JTAG chain configuration.

`verify_jtag (enable|disable)` [Command]

> Enables verification of DR and IR scans, to help detect programming errors. For IR scans, `verify_ircapture` must also be enabled. Default is enabled.

17.2 TAP state names

The *tap_state* names used by OpenOCD in the **drscan**, **irscan**, and **pathmove** commands are the same as those used in SVF boundary scan documents, except that SVF uses IDLE instead of RUN/IDLE.

- **RESET** ... *stable* (with TMS high); acts as if TRST were pulsed
- **RUN/IDLE** ... *stable*; don't assume this always means IDLE
- **DRSELECT**
- **DRCAPTURE**
- **DRSHIFT** ... *stable*; TDI/TDO shifting through the data register
- **DREXIT1**
- **DRPAUSE** ... *stable*; data register ready for update or more shifting
- **DREXIT2**
- **DRUPDATE**
- **IRSELECT**
- **IRCAPTURE**
- **IRSHIFT** ... *stable*; TDI/TDO shifting through the instruction register
- **IREXIT1**
- **IRPAUSE** ... *stable*; instruction register ready for update or more shifting
- **IREXIT2**
- **IRUPDATE**

Note that only six of those states are fully "stable" in the face of TMS fixed (low except for RESET) and a free-running JTAG clock. For all the others, the next TCK transition changes to a new state.

- From DRSHIFT and IRSHIFT, clock transitions will produce side effects by changing register contents. The values to be latched in upcoming DRUPDATE or IRUPDATE states may not be as expected.
- RUN/IDLE, DRPAUSE, and IRPAUSE are reasonable choices after **drscan** or **irscan** commands, since they are free of JTAG side effects.
- RUN/IDLE may have side effects that appear at non-JTAG levels, such as advancing the ARM9E-S instruction pipeline. Consult the documentation for the TAP(s) you are working with.

18 Boundary Scan Commands

One of the original purposes of JTAG was to support boundary scan based hardware testing. Although its primary focus is to support On-Chip Debugging, OpenOCD also includes some boundary scan commands.

18.1 SVF: Serial Vector Format

The Serial Vector Format, better known as *SVF*, is a way to represent JTAG test patterns in text files. In a debug session using JTAG for its transport protocol, OpenOCD supports running such test files.

svf *filename* [quiet]   [Command]
> This issues a JTAG reset (Test-Logic-Reset) and then runs the SVF script from **filename**. Unless the **quiet** option is specified, each command is logged before it is executed.

18.2 XSVF: Xilinx Serial Vector Format

The Xilinx Serial Vector Format, better known as *XSVF*, is a binary representation of SVF which is optimized for use with Xilinx devices. In a debug session using JTAG for its transport protocol, OpenOCD supports running such test files.

> **Important:** Not all XSVF commands are supported.

xsvf (*tapname*|plain) *filename* [virt2] [quiet]   [Command]
> This issues a JTAG reset (Test-Logic-Reset) and then runs the XSVF script from **filename**. When a *tapname* is specified, the commands are directed at that TAP. When **virt2** is specified, the XRUNTEST command counts are interpreted as TCK cycles instead of microseconds. Unless the **quiet** option is specified, messages are logged for comments and some retries.

The OpenOCD sources also include two utility scripts for working with XSVF; they are not currently installed after building the software. You may find them useful:

- *svf2xsvf* ... converts SVF files into the extended XSVF syntax understood by the **xsvf** command; see notes below.
- *xsvfdump* ... converts XSVF files into a text output format; understands the OpenOCD extensions.

The input format accepts a handful of non-standard extensions. These include three opcodes corresponding to SVF extensions from Lattice Semiconductor (LCOUNT, LDELAY, LDSR), and two opcodes supporting a more accurate translation of SVF (XTRST, XWAIT-STATE). If *xsvfdump* shows a file is using those opcodes, it probably will not be usable with other XSVF tools.

19 Utility Commands

19.1 RAM testing

There is often a need to stress-test random access memory (RAM) for errors. OpenOCD comes with a Tcl implementation of well-known memory testing procedures allowing the detection of all sorts of issues with electrical wiring, defective chips, PCB layout and other common hardware problems.

To use them, you usually need to initialise your RAM controller first; consult your SoC's documentation to get the recommended list of register operations and translate them to the corresponding `mww`/`mwb` commands.

Load the memory testing functions with

```
source [find tools/memtest.tcl]
```

to get access to the following facilities:

`memTestDataBus` *address*   [Command]
> Test the data bus wiring in a memory region by performing a walking 1's test at a fixed address within that region.

`memTestAddressBus` *baseaddress size*   [Command]
> Perform a walking 1's test on the relevant bits of the address and check for aliasing. This test will find single-bit address failures such as stuck-high, stuck-low, and shorted pins.

`memTestDevice` *baseaddress size*   [Command]
> Test the integrity of a physical memory device by performing an increment/decrement test over the entire region. In the process every storage bit in the device is tested as zero and as one.

`runAllMemTests` *baseaddress size*   [Command]
> Run all of the above tests over a specified memory region.

19.2 Firmware recovery helpers

OpenOCD includes an easy-to-use script to facilitate mass-market devices recovery with JTAG.

For quickstart instructions run:

```
openocd -f tools/firmware-recovery.tcl -c firmware_help
```

20 TFTP

If OpenOCD runs on an embedded host (as ZY1000 does), then TFTP can be used to access files on PCs (either the developer's PC or some other PC).

The way this works on the ZY1000 is to prefix a filename by "/tftp/ip/" and append the TFTP path on the TFTP server (tftpd). For example,

```
load_image /tftp/10.0.0.96/c:\temp\abc.elf
```

will load c:\temp\abc.elf from the developer pc (10.0.0.96) into memory as if the file was hosted on the embedded host.

In order to achieve decent performance, you must choose a TFTP server that supports a packet size bigger than the default packet size (512 bytes). There are numerous TFTP servers out there (free and commercial) and you will have to do a bit of googling to find something that fits your requirements.

21 GDB and OpenOCD

OpenOCD complies with the remote gdbserver protocol and, as such, can be used to debug remote targets. Setting up GDB to work with OpenOCD can involve several components:

- The OpenOCD server support for GDB may need to be configured. See [GDB Configuration], page 33.
- GDB's support for OpenOCD may need configuration, as shown in this chapter.
- If you have a GUI environment like Eclipse, that also will probably need to be configured.

Of course, the version of GDB you use will need to be one which has been built to know about the target CPU you're using. It's probably part of the tool chain you're using. For example, if you are doing cross-development for ARM on an x86 PC, instead of using the native x86 `gdb` command you might use `arm-none-eabi-gdb` if that's the tool chain used to compile your code.

21.1 Connecting to GDB

Use GDB 6.7 or newer with OpenOCD if you run into trouble. For instance GDB 6.3 has a known bug that produces bogus memory access errors, which has since been fixed; see `http://osdir.com/ml/gdb.bugs.discuss/2004-12/msg00018.html`

OpenOCD can communicate with GDB in two ways:

1. A socket (TCP/IP) connection is typically started as follows:

   `target remote localhost:3333`

   This would cause GDB to connect to the gdbserver on the local pc using port 3333.

   It is also possible to use the GDB extended remote protocol as follows:

   `target extended-remote localhost:3333`

2. A pipe connection is typically started as follows:

   `target remote | openocd -c "gdb_port pipe; log_output openocd.log"`

   This would cause GDB to run OpenOCD and communicate using pipes (stdin/stdout). Using this method has the advantage of GDB starting/stopping OpenOCD for the debug session. log_output sends the log output to a file to ensure that the pipe is not saturated when using higher debug level outputs.

To list the available OpenOCD commands type `monitor help` on the GDB command line.

21.2 Sample GDB session startup

With the remote protocol, GDB sessions start a little differently than they do when you're debugging locally. Here's an example showing how to start a debug session with a small ARM program. In this case the program was linked to be loaded into SRAM on a Cortex-M3. Most programs would be written into flash (address 0) and run from there.

```
$ arm-none-eabi-gdb example.elf
(gdb) target remote localhost:3333
Remote debugging using localhost:3333
...
```

```
(gdb) monitor reset halt
...
(gdb) load
Loading section .vectors, size 0x100 lma 0x20000000
Loading section .text, size 0x5a0 lma 0x20000100
Loading section .data, size 0x18 lma 0x200006a0
Start address 0x2000061c, load size 1720
Transfer rate: 22 KB/sec, 573 bytes/write.
(gdb) continue
Continuing.
...
```

You could then interrupt the GDB session to make the program break, type `where` to show the stack, `list` to show the code around the program counter, `step` through code, set breakpoints or watchpoints, and so on.

21.3 Configuring GDB for OpenOCD

OpenOCD supports the gdb `qSupported` packet, this enables information to be sent by the GDB remote server (i.e. OpenOCD) to GDB. Typical information includes packet size and the device's memory map. You do not need to configure the packet size by hand, and the relevant parts of the memory map should be automatically set up when you declare (NOR) flash banks.

However, there are other things which GDB can't currently query. You may need to set those up by hand. As OpenOCD starts up, you will often see a line reporting something like:

```
Info : lm3s.cpu: hardware has 6 breakpoints, 4 watchpoints
```

You can pass that information to GDB with these commands:

```
set remote hardware-breakpoint-limit 6
set remote hardware-watchpoint-limit 4
```

With that particular hardware (Cortex-M3) the hardware breakpoints only work for code running from flash memory. Most other ARM systems do not have such restrictions.

Another example of useful GDB configuration came from a user who found that single stepping his Cortex-M3 didn't work well with IRQs and an RTOS until he told GDB to disable the IRQs while stepping:

```
define hook-step
mon cortex_m maskisr on
end
define hookpost-step
mon cortex_m maskisr off
end
```

Rather than typing such commands interactively, you may prefer to save them in a file and have GDB execute them as it starts, perhaps using a `.gdbinit` in your project directory or starting GDB using `gdb -x filename`.

21.4 Programming using GDB

By default the target memory map is sent to GDB. This can be disabled by the following OpenOCD configuration option:

```
gdb_memory_map disable
```

For this to function correctly a valid flash configuration must also be set in OpenOCD. For faster performance you should also configure a valid working area.

Informing GDB of the memory map of the target will enable GDB to protect any flash areas of the target and use hardware breakpoints by default. This means that the OpenOCD option `gdb_breakpoint_override` is not required when using a memory map. See [gdb_breakpoint_override], page 33.

To view the configured memory map in GDB, use the GDB command `info mem`. All other unassigned addresses within GDB are treated as RAM.

GDB 6.8 and higher set any memory area not in the memory map as inaccessible. This can be changed to the old behaviour by using the following GDB command

```
set mem inaccessible-by-default off
```

If `gdb_flash_program enable` is also used, GDB will be able to program any flash memory using the vFlash interface.

GDB will look at the target memory map when a load command is given, if any areas to be programmed lie within the target flash area the vFlash packets will be used.

If the target needs configuring before GDB programming, an event script can be executed:

```
$_TARGETNAME configure -event EVENTNAME BODY
```

To verify any flash programming the GDB command `compare-sections` can be used.

21.5 Using OpenOCD SMP with GDB

For SMP support following GDB serial protocol packet have been defined :

- j - smp status request
- J - smp set request

OpenOCD implements :

- `jc` packet for reading core id displayed by GDB connection. Reply is XXXXXXXX (8 hex digits giving core id) or E01 for target not smp.
- JcXXXXXXXX (8 hex digits) packet for setting core id displayed at next GDB continue (core id -1 is reserved for returning to normal resume mode). Reply E01 for target not smp or OK on success.

Handling of this packet within GDB can be done :

- by the creation of an internal variable (i.e `_core`) by mean of function allocate_computed_value allowing following GDB command.

```
set $_core 1
#Jc01 packet is sent
print $_core
#jc packet is sent and result is affected in $
```

- by the usage of GDB maintenance command as described in following example (2 cpus in SMP with core id 0 and 1 see [Define CPU targets working in SMP], page 27).

```
# toggle0 : force display of coreid 0
define toggle0
maint packet Jc0
continue
main packet Jc-1
end
# toggle1 : force display of coreid 1
define toggle1
maint packet Jc1
continue
main packet Jc-1
end
```

21.6 RTOS Support

OpenOCD includes RTOS support, this will however need enabling as it defaults to disabled. It can be enabled by passing **-rtos** arg to the target See [RTOS Type], page 64.

An example setup is below:

```
$_TARGETNAME configure -rtos auto
```

This will attempt to auto detect the RTOS within your application.

Currently supported rtos's include:

- eCos
- ThreadX
- FreeRTOS
- linux
- ChibiOS
- embKernel
- mqx

  Note: Before an RTOS can be detected, it must export certain symbols; otherwise, it cannot be used by OpenOCD. Below is a list of the required symbols for each supported RTOS.

eCos symbols

Cyg_Thread::thread_list, Cyg_Scheduler_Base::current_thread.

ThreadX symbols

_tx_thread_current_ptr, _tx_thread_created_ptr, _tx_thread_created_count.

FreeRTOS symbols

pxCurrentTCB, pxReadyTasksLists, xDelayedTaskList1, xDelayedTaskList2, pxDelayedTaskList, pxOverflowDelayedTaskList, xPendingReadyList, uxCurrentNumberOfTasks, uxTopUsedPriority.

linux symbols
> init_task.

ChibiOS symbols
> rlist, ch_debug, chSysInit.

embKernel symbols
> Rtos::sCurrentTask, Rtos::sListReady, Rtos::sListSleep, Rtos::sListSuspended, Rtos::sMaxPriorities, Rtos::sCurrentTaskCount.

mqx symbols
> _mqx_kernel_data, MQX_init_struct.

For most RTOS supported the above symbols will be exported by default. However for some, eg. FreeRTOS, extra steps must be taken.

These RTOSes may require additional OpenOCD-specific file to be linked along with the project:

FreeRTOS   contrib/rtos-helpers/FreeRTOS-openocd.c

22 Tcl Scripting API

22.1 API rules

Tcl commands are stateless; e.g. the `telnet` command has a concept of currently active target, the Tcl API proc's take this sort of state information as an argument to each proc.

There are three main types of return values: single value, name value pair list and lists.

Name value pair. The proc 'foo' below returns a name/value pair list.

```
> set foo(me)  Duane
> set foo(you) Oyvind
> set foo(mouse) Micky
> set foo(duck) Donald
```

If one does this:

```
> set foo
```

The result is:

```
me Duane you Oyvind mouse Micky duck Donald
```

Thus, to get the names of the associative array is easy:

```
foreach { name value } [set foo] {
        puts "Name: $name, Value: $value"
}
```

Lists returned should be relatively small. Otherwise, a range should be passed in to the proc in question.

22.2 Internal low-level Commands

By "low-level," we mean commands that a human would typically not invoke directly.

Some low-level commands need to be prefixed with "ocd_"; e.g. `ocd_flash_banks` is the low-level API upon which `flash banks` is implemented.

- **mem2array** <*varname*> <*width*> <*addr*> <*nelems*>

  Read memory and return as a Tcl array for script processing

- **array2mem** <*varname*> <*width*> <*addr*> <*nelems*>

  Convert a Tcl array to memory locations and write the values

- **ocd_flash_banks** <*driver*> <*base*> <*size*> <*chip_width*> <*bus_width*> <*target*> [driver options ...]

  Return information about the flash banks

- **capture** <*command*>

  Run <*command*> and return full log output that was produced during its execution. Example:

  ```
  > capture "reset init"
  ```

OpenOCD commands can consist of two words, e.g. "flash banks". The `startup.tcl` "unknown" proc will translate this into a Tcl proc called "flash_banks".

22.3 OpenOCD specific Global Variables

Real Tcl has ::tcl_platform(), and platform::identify, and many other variables. JimTCL, as implemented in OpenOCD creates $ocd_HOSTOS which holds one of the following values:

- **cygwin** Running under Cygwin
- **darwin** Darwin (Mac-OS) is the underlying operating sytem.
- **freebsd** Running under FreeBSD
- **openbsd** Running under OpenBSD
- **netbsd** Running under NetBSD
- **linux** Linux is the underlying operating sytem
- **mingw32** Running under MingW32
- **winxx** Built using Microsoft Visual Studio
- **ecos** Running under eCos
- **other** Unknown, none of the above.

Note: 'winxx' was choosen because today (March-2009) no distinction is made between Win32 and Win64.

> **Note:** We should add support for a variable like Tcl variable `tcl_platform(platform)`, it should be called `jim_platform` (because it is jim, not real tcl).

22.4 Tcl RPC server

OpenOCD provides a simple RPC server that allows to run arbitrary Tcl commands and receive the results.

To access it, your application needs to connect to a configured TCP port (see `tcl_port`). Then it can pass any string to the interpreter terminating it with `0x1a` and wait for the return value (it will be terminated with `0x1a` as well). This can be repeated as many times as desired without reopening the connection.

Remember that most of the OpenOCD commands need to be prefixed with `ocd_` to get the results back. Sometimes you might also need the **capture** command.

See `contrib/rpc_examples/` for specific client implementations.

22.5 Tcl RPC server notifications

Notifications are sent asynchronously to other commands being executed over the RPC server, so the port must be polled continuously.

Target event, state and reset notifications are emitted as Tcl associative arrays in the following format.

```
type target_event event [event-name]
type target_state state [state-name]
type target_reset mode [reset-mode]
```

`tcl_notifications` [*on/off*]   [Command]
> Toggle output of target notifications to the current Tcl RPC server. Only available from the Tcl RPC server. Defaults to off.

22.6 Tcl RPC server trace output

Trace data is sent asynchronously to other commands being executed over the RPC server, so the port must be polled continuously.

Target trace data is emitted as a Tcl associative array in the following format.

```
type target_trace data [trace-data-hex-encoded]
```

tcl_trace [*on/off*]   [Command]

    Toggle output of target trace data to the current Tcl RPC server. Only available from the Tcl RPC server. Defaults to off.

    See an example application here: https: / / github . com / apmorton / OpenOcdTraceUtil [OpenOcdTraceUtil]

23 FAQ

1. **RTCK, also known as: Adaptive Clocking - What is it?**

In digital circuit design it is often refered to as "clock synchronisation" the JTAG interface uses one clock (TCK or TCLK) operating at some speed, your CPU target is operating at another. The two clocks are not synchronised, they are "asynchronous"

In order for the two to work together they must be synchronised well enough to work; JTAG can't go ten times faster than the CPU, for example. There are 2 basic options:

1. Use a special "adaptive clocking" circuit to change the JTAG clock rate to match what the CPU currently supports.
2. The JTAG clock must be fixed at some speed that's enough slower than the CPU clock that all TMS and TDI transitions can be detected.

Does this really matter? For some chips and some situations, this is a non-issue, like a 500MHz ARM926 with a 5 MHz JTAG link; the CPU has no difficulty keeping up with JTAG. Startup sequences are often problematic though, as are other situations where the CPU clock rate changes (perhaps to save power).

For example, Atmel AT91SAM chips start operation from reset with a 32kHz system clock. Boot firmware may activate the main oscillator and PLL before switching to a faster clock (perhaps that 500 MHz ARM926 scenario). If you're using JTAG to debug that startup sequence, you must slow the JTAG clock to sometimes 1 to 4kHz. After startup completes, JTAG can use a faster clock.

Consider also debugging a 500MHz ARM926 hand held battery powered device that enters a low power "deep sleep" mode, at 32kHz CPU clock, between keystrokes unless it has work to do. When would that 5 MHz JTAG clock be usable?

Solution #1 - A special circuit

In order to make use of this, your CPU, board, and JTAG adapter must all support the RTCK feature. Not all of them support this; keep reading!

The RTCK ("Return TCK") signal in some ARM chips is used to help with this problem. ARM has a good description of the problem described at this link: http://www.arm.com/support/faqdev/4170.html [checked 28/nov/2008]. Link title: "How does the JTAG synchronisation logic work? / how does adaptive clocking work?".

The nice thing about adaptive clocking is that "battery powered hand held device example" - the adaptiveness works perfectly all the time. One can set a break point or halt the system in the deep power down code, slow step out until the system speeds up.

Note that adaptive clocking may also need to work at the board level, when a board-level scan chain has multiple chips. Parallel clock voting schemes are good way to implement this, both within and between chips, and can easily be implemented with a CPLD. It's not difficult to have logic fan a module's input TCK signal out to each TAP in the scan chain, and then wait until each TAP's RTCK comes back with the right polarity before changing the output RTCK signal. Texas Instruments makes some clock voting logic available for free (with no support) in VHDL form; see http://tiexpressdsp.com/index.php/Adaptive_Clocking

Solution #2 - Always works - but may be slower

Often this is a perfectly acceptable solution.

In most simple terms: Often the JTAG clock must be 1/10 to 1/12 of the target clock speed. But what that "magic division" is varies depending on the chips on your board. **ARM rule of thumb** Most ARM based systems require an 6:1 division; ARM11 cores use an 8:1 division. **Xilinx rule of thumb** is 1/12 the clock speed.

Note: most full speed FT2232 based JTAG adapters are limited to a maximum of 6MHz. The ones using USB high speed chips (FT2232H) often support faster clock rates (and adaptive clocking).

You can still debug the 'low power' situations - you just need to either use a fixed and very slow JTAG clock rate ... or else manually adjust the clock speed at every step. (Adjusting is painful and tedious, and is not always practical.)

It is however easy to "code your way around it" - i.e.: Cheat a little, have a special debug mode in your application that does a "high power sleep". If you are careful - 98% of your problems can be debugged this way.

Note that on ARM you may need to avoid using the *wait for interrupt* operation in your idle loops even if you don't otherwise change the CPU clock rate. That operation gates the CPU clock, and thus the JTAG clock; which prevents JTAG access. One consequence is not being able to **halt** cores which are executing that *wait for interrupt* operation.

To set the JTAG frequency use the command:

```
# Example: 1.234MHz
adapter_khz 1234
```

2. **Win32 Pathnames** Why don't backslashes work in Windows paths?

   OpenOCD uses Tcl and a backslash is an escape char. Use { and } around Windows filenames.

   ```
   > echo \a

   > echo {\a}
   \a
   > echo "\a"

   >
   ```

3. **Missing: cygwin1.dll** OpenOCD complains about a missing cygwin1.dll.

   Make sure you have Cygwin installed, or at least a version of OpenOCD that claims to come with all the necessary DLLs. When using Cygwin, try launching OpenOCD from the Cygwin shell.

4. **Breakpoint Issue** I'm trying to set a breakpoint using GDB (or a frontend like Insight or Eclipse), but OpenOCD complains that "Info: arm7_9_common.c:213 arm7_9_add_breakpoint(): sw breakpoint requested, but software breakpoints not enabled".

   GDB issues software breakpoints when a normal breakpoint is requested, or to implement source-line single-stepping. On ARMv4T systems, like ARM7TDMI, ARM720T or ARM920T, software breakpoints consume one of the two available hardware breakpoints.

5. **LPC2000 Flash** When erasing or writing LPC2000 on-chip flash, the operation fails at random.

   Make sure the core frequency specified in the `flash lpc2000` line matches the clock at the time you're programming the flash. If you've specified the crystal's frequency, make sure the PLL is disabled. If you've specified the full core speed (e.g. 60MHz), make sure the PLL is enabled.

6. **Amontec Chameleon** When debugging using an Amontec Chameleon in its JTAG Accelerator configuration, I keep getting "Error: amt_jtagaccel.c:184 amt_wait_scan_busy(): amt_jtagaccel timed out while waiting for end of scan, rtck was disabled".

   Make sure your PC's parallel port operates in EPP mode. You might have to try several settings in your PC BIOS (ECP, EPP, and different versions of those).

7. **Data Aborts** When debugging with OpenOCD and GDB (plain GDB, Insight, or Eclipse), I get lots of "Error: arm7_9_common.c:1771 arm7_9_read_memory(): memory read caused data abort".

   The errors are non-fatal, and are the result of GDB trying to trace stack frames beyond the last valid frame. It might be possible to prevent this by setting up a proper "initial" stack frame, if you happen to know what exactly has to be done, feel free to add this here.

   Simple: In your startup code - push 8 registers of zeros onto the stack before calling main(). What GDB is doing is "climbing" the run time stack by reading various values on the stack using the standard call frame for the target. GDB keeps going - until one of 2 things happen **#1** an invalid frame is found, or **#2** some huge number of stackframes have been processed. By pushing zeros on the stack, GDB gracefully stops.

   Debugging Interrupt Service Routines - In your ISR before you call your C code, do the same - artifically push some zeros onto the stack, remember to pop them off when the ISR is done.

   Also note: If you have a multi-threaded operating system, they often do not **in the intrest of saving memory** waste these few bytes. Painful...

8. **JTAG Reset Config** I get the following message in the OpenOCD console (or log file): "Warning: arm7_9_common.c:679 arm7_9_assert_reset(): srst resets test logic, too".

   This warning doesn't indicate any serious problem, as long as you don't want to debug your core right out of reset. Your .cfg file specified `jtag_reset trst_and_srst srst_pulls_trst` to tell OpenOCD that either your board, your debugger or your target uC (e.g. LPC2000) can't assert the two reset signals independently. With this setup, it's not possible to halt the core right out of reset, everything else should work fine.

9. **USB Power** When using OpenOCD in conjunction with Amontec JTAGkey and the Yagarto toolchain (Eclipse, arm-elf-gcc, arm-elf-gdb), the debugging seems to be unstable. When single-stepping over large blocks of code, GDB and OpenOCD quit with an error message. Is there a stability issue with OpenOCD?

   No, this is not a stability issue concerning OpenOCD. Most users have solved this issue by simply using a self-powered USB hub, which they connect their Amontec JTAGkey to. Apparently, some computers do not provide a USB power supply stable enough for the Amontec JTAGkey to be operated.

Laptops running on battery have this problem too...

10. **USB Power** When using the Amontec JTAGkey, sometimes OpenOCD crashes with the following error messages: "Error: ft2232.c:201 ft2232_read(): FT_Read returned: 4" and "Error: ft2232.c:365 ft2232_send_and_recv(): couldn't read from FT2232". What does that mean and what might be the reason for this?

    First of all, the reason might be the USB power supply. Try using a self-powered hub instead of a direct connection to your computer. Secondly, the error code 4 corresponds to an FT_IO_ERROR, which means that the driver for the FTDI USB chip ran into some sort of error - this points us to a USB problem.

11. **GDB Disconnects** When using the Amontec JTAGkey, sometimes OpenOCD crashes with the following error message: "Error: gdb_server.c:101 gdb_get_char(): read: 10054". What does that mean and what might be the reason for this?

    Error code 10054 corresponds to WSAECONNRESET, which means that the debugger (GDB) has closed the connection to OpenOCD. This might be a GDB issue.

12. **LPC2000 Flash** In the configuration file in the section where flash device configurations are described, there is a parameter for specifying the clock frequency for LPC2000 internal flash devices (e.g. `flash bank $_FLASHNAME lpc2000 0x0 0x40000 0 0 $_TARGETNAME lpc2000_v1 14746 calc_checksum`), which must be specified in kilohertz. However, I do have a quartz crystal of a frequency that contains fractions of kilohertz (e.g. 14,745,600 Hz, i.e. 14,745.600 kHz). Is it possible to specify real numbers for the clock frequency?

    No. The clock frequency specified here must be given as an integral number. However, this clock frequency is used by the In-Application-Programming (IAP) routines of the LPC2000 family only, which seems to be very tolerant concerning the given clock frequency, so a slight difference between the specified clock frequency and the actual clock frequency will not cause any trouble.

13. **Command Order** Do I have to keep a specific order for the commands in the configuration file?

    Well, yes and no. Commands can be given in arbitrary order, yet the devices listed for the JTAG scan chain must be given in the right order (jtag newdevice), with the device closest to the TDO-Pin being listed first. In general, whenever objects of the same type exist which require an index number, then these objects must be given in the right order (jtag newtap, targets and flash banks - a target references a jtag newtap and a flash bank references a target).

    You can use the "scan_chain" command to verify and display the tap order.

    Also, some commands can't execute until after **init** has been processed. Such commands include **nand probe** and everything else that needs to write to controller registers, perhaps for setting up DRAM and loading it with code.

14. **JTAG TAP Order** Do I have to declare the TAPS in some particular order?

    Yes; whenever you have more than one, you must declare them in the same order used by the hardware.

    Many newer devices have multiple JTAG TAPs. For example: ST Microsystems STM32 chips have two TAPs, a "boundary scan TAP" and "Cortex-M3" TAP. Example: The STM32 reference manual, Document ID: RM0008, Section 26.5, Figure

259, page 651/681, the "TDI" pin is connected to the boundary scan TAP, which then connects to the Cortex-M3 TAP, which then connects to the TDO pin.

Thus, the proper order for the STM32 chip is: (1) The Cortex-M3, then (2) The boundary scan TAP. If your board includes an additional JTAG chip in the scan chain (for example a Xilinx CPLD or FPGA) you could place it before or after the STM32 chip in the chain. For example:

- OpenOCD_TDI(output) -> STM32 TDI Pin (BS Input)
- STM32 BS TDO (output) -> STM32 Cortex-M3 TDI (input)
- STM32 Cortex-M3 TDO (output) -> SM32 TDO Pin
- STM32 TDO Pin (output) -> Xilinx TDI Pin (input)
- Xilinx TDO Pin -> OpenOCD TDO (input)

The "jtag device" commands would thus be in the order shown below. Note:

- jtag newtap Xilinx tap -irlen ...
- jtag newtap stm32 cpu -irlen ...
- jtag newtap stm32 bs -irlen ...
- # Create the debug target and say where it is
- target create stm32.cpu -chain-position stm32.cpu ...

15. **SYSCOMP** Sometimes my debugging session terminates with an error. When I look into the log file, I can see these error messages: Error: arm7_9_common.c:561 arm7_9_execute_sys_speed(): timeout waiting for SYSCOMP

TODO.

24 Tcl Crash Course

Not everyone knows Tcl - this is not intended to be a replacement for learning Tcl, the intent of this chapter is to give you some idea of how the Tcl scripts work.

This chapter is written with two audiences in mind. (1) OpenOCD users who need to understand a bit more of how Jim-Tcl works so they can do something useful, and (2) those that want to add a new command to OpenOCD.

24.1 Tcl Rule #1

There is a famous joke, it goes like this:

1. Rule #1: The wife is always correct
2. Rule #2: If you think otherwise, See Rule #1

The Tcl equal is this:

1. Rule #1: Everything is a string
2. Rule #2: If you think otherwise, See Rule #1

As in the famous joke, the consequences of Rule #1 are profound. Once you understand Rule #1, you will understand Tcl.

24.2 Tcl Rule #1b

There is a second pair of rules.

1. Rule #1: Control flow does not exist. Only commands
   For example: the classic FOR loop or IF statement is not a control flow item, they are commands, there is no such thing as control flow in Tcl.
2. Rule #2: If you think otherwise, See Rule #1
   Actually what happens is this: There are commands that by convention, act like control flow key words in other languages. One of those commands is the word "for", another command is "if".

24.3 Per Rule #1 - All Results are strings

Every Tcl command results in a string. The word "result" is used deliberately. No result is just an empty string. Remember: *Rule #1 - Everything is a string*

24.4 Tcl Quoting Operators

In life of a Tcl script, there are two important periods of time, the difference is subtle.

1. Parse Time
2. Evaluation Time

The two key items here are how "quoted things" work in Tcl. Tcl has three primary quoting constructs, the [square-brackets] the {curly-braces} and "double-quotes"

By now you should know $VARIABLES always start with a $DOLLAR sign. BTW: To set a variable, you actually use the command "set", as in "set VARNAME VALUE" much like the ancient BASIC langauge "let x = 1" statement, but without the equal sign.

- **[square-brackets]**
  [square-brackets] are command substitutions. It operates much like Unix Shell 'back-ticks'. The result of a [square-bracket] operation is exactly 1 string. *Remember Rule #1 - Everything is a string.* These two statements are roughly identical:

  ```
  # bash example
  X='date'
  echo "The Date is: $X"
  # Tcl example
  set X [date]
  puts "The Date is: $X"
  ```

- **"double-quoted-things"**
  "double-quoted-things" are just simply quoted text. $VARIABLES and [square-brackets] are expanded in place - the result however is exactly 1 string. *Remember Rule #1 - Everything is a string*

  ```
  set x "Dinner"
  puts "It is now \"[date]\", $x is in 1 hour"
  ```

- **{Curly-Braces}**
  {Curly-Braces} are magic: $VARIABLES and [square-brackets] are parsed, but are NOT expanded or executed. {Curly-Braces} are like 'single-quote' operators in BASH shell scripts, with the added feature: {curly-braces} can be nested, single quotes can not. {{{this is nested 3 times}}} NOTE: [date] is a bad example; at this writing, Jim/OpenOCD does not have a date command.

24.5 Consequences of Rule 1/2/3/4

The consequences of Rule 1 are profound.

24.5.1 Tokenisation & Execution.

Of course, whitespace, blank lines and #comment lines are handled in the normal way.

As a script is parsed, each (multi) line in the script file is tokenised and according to the quoting rules. After tokenisation, that line is immedatly executed.

Multi line statements end with one or more "still-open" {curly-braces} which - eventually - closes a few lines later.

24.5.2 Command Execution

Remember earlier: There are no "control flow" statements in Tcl. Instead there are COMMANDS that simply act like control flow operators.

Commands are executed like this:

1. Parse the next line into (argc) and (argv[]).

2. Look up (argv[0]) in a table and call its function.

3. Repeat until End Of File.

It sort of works like this:

```
for(;;){
    ReadAndParse( &argc, &argv );
```

```
        cmdPtr = LookupCommand( argv[0] );

        (*cmdPtr->Execute)( argc, argv );
    }
```

When the command "proc" is parsed (which creates a procedure function) it gets 3 parameters on the command line. **1** the name of the proc (function), **2** the list of parameters, and **3** the body of the function. Not the choice of words: LIST and BODY. The PROC command stores these items in a table somewhere so it can be found by "LookupCommand()"

24.5.3 The FOR command

The most interesting command to look at is the FOR command. In Tcl, the FOR command is normally implemented in C. Remember, FOR is a command just like any other command.

When the ascii text containing the FOR command is parsed, the parser produces 5 parameter strings, *(If in doubt: Refer to Rule #1)* they are:

0. The ascii text 'for'

1. The start text

2. The test expression

3. The next text

4. The body text

Sort of reminds you of "main(int argc, char **argv)" does it not? Remember *Rule #1 - Everything is a string.* The key point is this: Often many of those parameters are in {curly-braces} - thus the variables inside are not expanded or replaced until later.

Remember that every Tcl command looks like the classic "main(argc, argv)" function in C. In JimTCL - they actually look like this:

```
int
MyCommand( Jim_Interp *interp,
           int *argc,
           Jim_Obj * const *argvs );
```

Real Tcl is nearly identical. Although the newer versions have introduced a byte-code parser and intepreter, but at the core, it still operates in the same basic way.

24.5.4 FOR command implementation

To understand Tcl it is perhaps most helpful to see the FOR command. Remember, it is a COMMAND not a control flow structure.

In Tcl there are two underlying C helper functions.

Remember Rule #1 - You are a string.

The **first** helper parses and executes commands found in an ascii string. Commands can be seperated by semicolons, or newlines. While parsing, variables are expanded via the quoting rules.

The **second** helper evaluates an ascii string as a numerical expression and returns a value.

Here is an example of how the **FOR** command could be implemented. The pseudo code below does not show error handling.

```
    void Execute_AsciiString( void *interp, const char *string );

    int Evaluate_AsciiExpression( void *interp, const char *string );

    int
    MyForCommand( void *interp,
                  int argc,
                  char **argv )
    {
       if( argc != 5 ){
           SetResult( interp, "WRONG number of parameters");
           return ERROR;
       }

       // argv[0] = the ascii string just like C

       // Execute the start statement.
       Execute_AsciiString( interp, argv[1] );

       // Top of loop test
       for(;;){
           i = Evaluate_AsciiExpression(interp, argv[2]);
           if( i == 0 )
               break;

           // Execute the body
           Execute_AsciiString( interp, argv[3] );

           // Execute the LOOP part
           Execute_AsciiString( interp, argv[4] );
       }

       // Return no error
       SetResult( interp, "" );
       return SUCCESS;
    }
```

Every other command IF, WHILE, FORMAT, PUTS, EXPR, everything works in the same basic way.

24.6 OpenOCD Tcl Usage

24.6.1 source and find commands

Where: In many configuration files
Example: **source [find FILENAME]**
Remember the parsing rules

1. The **find** command is in square brackets, and is executed with the parameter FILE-

NAME. It should find and return the full path to a file with that name; it uses an internal search path. The RESULT is a string, which is substituted into the command line in place of the bracketed `find` command. (Don't try to use a FILENAME which includes the "#" character. That character begins Tcl comments.)

2. The `source` command is executed with the resulting filename; it reads a file and executes as a script.

24.6.2 format command

Where: Generally occurs in numerous places.

Tcl has no command like **printf()**, instead it has **format**, which is really more like **sprintf()**.

Example

```
set x 6
set y 7
puts [format "The answer: %d" [expr $x * $y]]
```

1. The SET command creates 2 variables, X and Y.

2. The double [nested] EXPR command performs math
   The EXPR command produces numerical result as a string.
   Refer to Rule #1

3. The format command is executed, producing a single string
   Refer to Rule #1.

4. The PUTS command outputs the text.

24.6.3 Body or Inlined Text

Where: Various TARGET scripts.

```
#1 Good
   proc someproc {} {
       ... multiple lines of stuff ...
   }
   $_TARGETNAME configure -event FOO someproc
#2 Good - no variables
   $_TARGETNAME confgure -event foo "this ; that;"
#3 Good Curly Braces
   $_TARGETNAME configure -event FOO {
       puts "Time: [date]"
   }
#4 DANGER DANGER DANGER
   $_TARGETNAME configure -event foo "puts \"Time: [date]\""
```

1. The $_TARGETNAME is an OpenOCD variable convention.
   $_TARGETNAME represents the last target created, the value changes each time a new target is created. Remember the parsing rules. When the ascii text is parsed, the **$_TARGETNAME** becomes a simple string, the name of the target which happens to be a TARGET (object) command.

2. The 2nd parameter to the **-event** parameter is a TCBODY
   There are 4 examples:

1. The TCLBODY is a simple string that happens to be a proc name
2. The TCLBODY is several simple commands seperated by semicolons
3. The TCLBODY is a multi-line {curly-brace} quoted string
4. The TCLBODY is a string with variables that get expanded.

In the end, when the target event FOO occurs the TCLBODY is evaluated. Method **#1** and **#2** are functionally identical. For Method **#3** and **#4** it is more interesting. What is the TCLBODY?

Remember the parsing rules. In case #3, {curly-braces} mean the $VARS and [square-brackets] are expanded later, when the EVENT occurs, and the text is evaluated. In case #4, they are replaced before the "Target Object Command" is executed. This occurs at the same time $_TARGETNAME is replaced. In case #4 the date will never change. {BTW: [date] is a bad example; at this writing, Jim/OpenOCD does not have a date command}

24.6.4 Global Variables

Where: You might discover this when writing your own procs
In simple terms: Inside a PROC, if you need to access a global variable you must say so. See also "upvar". Example:

```
proc myproc { } {
      set y 0 #Local variable Y
      global x #Global variable X
      puts [format "X=%d, Y=%d" $x $y]
}
```

24.7 Other Tcl Hacks

Dynamic variable creation

```
# Dynamically create a bunch of variables.
for { set x 0 } { $x < 32 } { set x [expr $x + 1]} {
    # Create var name
    set vn [format "BIT%d" $x]
    # Make it a global
    global $vn
    # Set it.
    set $vn [expr (1 << $x)]
}
```

Dynamic proc/command creation

```
# One "X" function - 5 uart functions.
foreach who {A B C D E}
   proc [format "show_uart%c" $who] { } "show_UARTx $who"
}
```

Appendix A The GNU Free Documentation License.

Version 1.2, November 2002

Copyright © 2000,2001,2002 Free Software Foundation, Inc.
51 Franklin St, Fifth Floor, Boston, MA 02110-1301, USA

0. PREAMBLE

The purpose of this License is to make a manual, textbook, or other functional and useful document *free* in the sense of freedom: to assure everyone the effective freedom to copy and redistribute it, with or without modifying it, either commercially or non-commercially. Secondarily, this License preserves for the author and publisher a way to get credit for their work, while not being considered responsible for modifications made by others.

This License is a kind of "copyleft", which means that derivative works of the document must themselves be free in the same sense. It complements the GNU General Public License, which is a copyleft license designed for free software.

We have designed this License in order to use it for manuals for free software, because free software needs free documentation: a free program should come with manuals providing the same freedoms that the software does. But this License is not limited to software manuals; it can be used for any textual work, regardless of subject matter or whether it is published as a printed book. We recommend this License principally for works whose purpose is instruction or reference.

1. APPLICABILITY AND DEFINITIONS

This License applies to any manual or other work, in any medium, that contains a notice placed by the copyright holder saying it can be distributed under the terms of this License. Such a notice grants a world-wide, royalty-free license, unlimited in duration, to use that work under the conditions stated herein. The "Document", below, refers to any such manual or work. Any member of the public is a licensee, and is addressed as "you". You accept the license if you copy, modify or distribute the work in a way requiring permission under copyright law.

A "Modified Version" of the Document means any work containing the Document or a portion of it, either copied verbatim, or with modifications and/or translated into another language.

A "Secondary Section" is a named appendix or a front-matter section of the Document that deals exclusively with the relationship of the publishers or authors of the Document to the Document's overall subject (or to related matters) and contains nothing that could fall directly within that overall subject. (Thus, if the Document is in part a textbook of mathematics, a Secondary Section may not explain any mathematics.) The relationship could be a matter of historical connection with the subject or with related matters, or of legal, commercial, philosophical, ethical or political position regarding them.

The "Invariant Sections" are certain Secondary Sections whose titles are designated, as being those of Invariant Sections, in the notice that says that the Document is released under this License. If a section does not fit the above definition of Secondary then it is not allowed to be designated as Invariant. The Document may contain zero Invariant Sections. If the Document does not identify any Invariant Sections then there are none.

The "Cover Texts" are certain short passages of text that are listed, as Front-Cover Texts or Back-Cover Texts, in the notice that says that the Document is released under this License. A Front-Cover Text may be at most 5 words, and a Back-Cover Text may be at most 25 words.

A "Transparent" copy of the Document means a machine-readable copy, represented in a format whose specification is available to the general public, that is suitable for revising the document straightforwardly with generic text editors or (for images composed of pixels) generic paint programs or (for drawings) some widely available drawing editor, and that is suitable for input to text formatters or for automatic translation to a variety of formats suitable for input to text formatters. A copy made in an otherwise Transparent file format whose markup, or absence of markup, has been arranged to thwart or discourage subsequent modification by readers is not Transparent. An image format is not Transparent if used for any substantial amount of text. A copy that is not "Transparent" is called "Opaque".

Examples of suitable formats for Transparent copies include plain ASCII without markup, Texinfo input format, LaTeX input format, SGML or XML using a publicly available DTD, and standard-conforming simple HTML, PostScript or PDF designed for human modification. Examples of transparent image formats include PNG, XCF and JPG. Opaque formats include proprietary formats that can be read and edited only by proprietary word processors, SGML or XML for which the DTD and/or processing tools are not generally available, and the machine-generated HTML, PostScript or PDF produced by some word processors for output purposes only.

The "Title Page" means, for a printed book, the title page itself, plus such following pages as are needed to hold, legibly, the material this License requires to appear in the title page. For works in formats which do not have any title page as such, "Title Page" means the text near the most prominent appearance of the work's title, preceding the beginning of the body of the text.

A section "Entitled XYZ" means a named subunit of the Document whose title either is precisely XYZ or contains XYZ in parentheses following text that translates XYZ in another language. (Here XYZ stands for a specific section name mentioned below, such as "Acknowledgements", "Dedications", "Endorsements", or "History".) To "Preserve the Title" of such a section when you modify the Document means that it remains a section "Entitled XYZ" according to this definition.

The Document may include Warranty Disclaimers next to the notice which states that this License applies to the Document. These Warranty Disclaimers are considered to be included by reference in this License, but only as regards disclaiming warranties: any other implication that these Warranty Disclaimers may have is void and has no effect on the meaning of this License.

2. VERBATIM COPYING

You may copy and distribute the Document in any medium, either commercially or noncommercially, provided that this License, the copyright notices, and the license notice saying this License applies to the Document are reproduced in all copies, and that you add no other conditions whatsoever to those of this License. You may not use technical measures to obstruct or control the reading or further copying of the copies you make or distribute. However, you may accept compensation in exchange for copies. If you distribute a large enough number of copies you must also follow the conditions in section 3.

You may also lend copies, under the same conditions stated above, and you may publicly display copies.

3. COPYING IN QUANTITY

If you publish printed copies (or copies in media that commonly have printed covers) of the Document, numbering more than 100, and the Document's license notice requires Cover Texts, you must enclose the copies in covers that carry, clearly and legibly, all these Cover Texts: Front-Cover Texts on the front cover, and Back-Cover Texts on the back cover. Both covers must also clearly and legibly identify you as the publisher of these copies. The front cover must present the full title with all words of the title equally prominent and visible. You may add other material on the covers in addition. Copying with changes limited to the covers, as long as they preserve the title of the Document and satisfy these conditions, can be treated as verbatim copying in other respects.

If the required texts for either cover are too voluminous to fit legibly, you should put the first ones listed (as many as fit reasonably) on the actual cover, and continue the rest onto adjacent pages.

If you publish or distribute Opaque copies of the Document numbering more than 100, you must either include a machine-readable Transparent copy along with each Opaque copy, or state in or with each Opaque copy a computer-network location from which the general network-using public has access to download using public-standard network protocols a complete Transparent copy of the Document, free of added material. If you use the latter option, you must take reasonably prudent steps, when you begin distribution of Opaque copies in quantity, to ensure that this Transparent copy will remain thus accessible at the stated location until at least one year after the last time you distribute an Opaque copy (directly or through your agents or retailers) of that edition to the public.

It is requested, but not required, that you contact the authors of the Document well before redistributing any large number of copies, to give them a chance to provide you with an updated version of the Document.

4. MODIFICATIONS

You may copy and distribute a Modified Version of the Document under the conditions of sections 2 and 3 above, provided that you release the Modified Version under precisely this License, with the Modified Version filling the role of the Document, thus licensing distribution and modification of the Modified Version to whoever possesses a copy of it. In addition, you must do these things in the Modified Version:

A. Use in the Title Page (and on the covers, if any) a title distinct from that of the Document, and from those of previous versions (which should, if there were any, be listed in the History section of the Document). You may use the same title as a previous version if the original publisher of that version gives permission.

B. List on the Title Page, as authors, one or more persons or entities responsible for authorship of the modifications in the Modified Version, together with at least five of the principal authors of the Document (all of its principal authors, if it has fewer than five), unless they release you from this requirement.

C. State on the Title page the name of the publisher of the Modified Version, as the publisher.

D. Preserve all the copyright notices of the Document.

E. Add an appropriate copyright notice for your modifications adjacent to the other copyright notices.

F. Include, immediately after the copyright notices, a license notice giving the public permission to use the Modified Version under the terms of this License, in the form shown in the Addendum below.

G. Preserve in that license notice the full lists of Invariant Sections and required Cover Texts given in the Document's license notice.

H. Include an unaltered copy of this License.

I. Preserve the section Entitled "History", Preserve its Title, and add to it an item stating at least the title, year, new authors, and publisher of the Modified Version as given on the Title Page. If there is no section Entitled "History" in the Document, create one stating the title, year, authors, and publisher of the Document as given on its Title Page, then add an item describing the Modified Version as stated in the previous sentence.

J. Preserve the network location, if any, given in the Document for public access to a Transparent copy of the Document, and likewise the network locations given in the Document for previous versions it was based on. These may be placed in the "History" section. You may omit a network location for a work that was published at least four years before the Document itself, or if the original publisher of the version it refers to gives permission.

K. For any section Entitled "Acknowledgements" or "Dedications", Preserve the Title of the section, and preserve in the section all the substance and tone of each of the contributor acknowledgements and/or dedications given therein.

L. Preserve all the Invariant Sections of the Document, unaltered in their text and in their titles. Section numbers or the equivalent are not considered part of the section titles.

M. Delete any section Entitled "Endorsements". Such a section may not be included in the Modified Version.

N. Do not retitle any existing section to be Entitled "Endorsements" or to conflict in title with any Invariant Section.

O. Preserve any Warranty Disclaimers.

If the Modified Version includes new front-matter sections or appendices that qualify as Secondary Sections and contain no material copied from the Document, you may at your option designate some or all of these sections as invariant. To do this, add their titles to the list of Invariant Sections in the Modified Version's license notice. These titles must be distinct from any other section titles.

You may add a section Entitled "Endorsements", provided it contains nothing but endorsements of your Modified Version by various parties—for example, statements of peer review or that the text has been approved by an organization as the authoritative definition of a standard.

You may add a passage of up to five words as a Front-Cover Text, and a passage of up to 25 words as a Back-Cover Text, to the end of the list of Cover Texts in the Modified Version. Only one passage of Front-Cover Text and one of Back-Cover Text may be added by (or through arrangements made by) any one entity. If the Document already includes a cover text for the same cover, previously added by you or by arrangement made by the same entity you are acting on behalf of, you may not add another; but you may replace the old one, on explicit permission from the previous publisher that added the old one.

The author(s) and publisher(s) of the Document do not by this License give permission to use their names for publicity for or to assert or imply endorsement of any Modified Version.

5. COMBINING DOCUMENTS

You may combine the Document with other documents released under this License, under the terms defined in section 4 above for modified versions, provided that you include in the combination all of the Invariant Sections of all of the original documents, unmodified, and list them all as Invariant Sections of your combined work in its license notice, and that you preserve all their Warranty Disclaimers.

The combined work need only contain one copy of this License, and multiple identical Invariant Sections may be replaced with a single copy. If there are multiple Invariant Sections with the same name but different contents, make the title of each such section unique by adding at the end of it, in parentheses, the name of the original author or publisher of that section if known, or else a unique number. Make the same adjustment to the section titles in the list of Invariant Sections in the license notice of the combined work.

In the combination, you must combine any sections Entitled "History" in the various original documents, forming one section Entitled "History"; likewise combine any sections Entitled "Acknowledgements", and any sections Entitled "Dedications". You must delete all sections Entitled "Endorsements."

6. COLLECTIONS OF DOCUMENTS

You may make a collection consisting of the Document and other documents released under this License, and replace the individual copies of this License in the various documents with a single copy that is included in the collection, provided that you follow the rules of this License for verbatim copying of each of the documents in all other respects.

You may extract a single document from such a collection, and distribute it individually under this License, provided you insert a copy of this License into the extracted document, and follow this License in all other respects regarding verbatim copying of that document.

7. AGGREGATION WITH INDEPENDENT WORKS

A compilation of the Document or its derivatives with other separate and independent documents or works, in or on a volume of a storage or distribution medium, is called an "aggregate" if the copyright resulting from the compilation is not used to limit the legal rights of the compilation's users beyond what the individual works permit. When the Document is included in an aggregate, this License does not apply to the other works in the aggregate which are not themselves derivative works of the Document.

If the Cover Text requirement of section 3 is applicable to these copies of the Document, then if the Document is less than one half of the entire aggregate, the Document's Cover Texts may be placed on covers that bracket the Document within the aggregate, or the electronic equivalent of covers if the Document is in electronic form. Otherwise they must appear on printed covers that bracket the whole aggregate.

8. TRANSLATION

Translation is considered a kind of modification, so you may distribute translations of the Document under the terms of section 4. Replacing Invariant Sections with translations requires special permission from their copyright holders, but you may include translations of some or all Invariant Sections in addition to the original versions of these Invariant Sections. You may include a translation of this License, and all the license notices in the Document, and any Warranty Disclaimers, provided that you also include the original English version of this License and the original versions of those notices and disclaimers. In case of a disagreement between the translation and the original version of this License or a notice or disclaimer, the original version will prevail.

If a section in the Document is Entitled "Acknowledgements", "Dedications", or "History", the requirement (section 4) to Preserve its Title (section 1) will typically require changing the actual title.

9. TERMINATION

You may not copy, modify, sublicense, or distribute the Document except as expressly provided for under this License. Any other attempt to copy, modify, sublicense or distribute the Document is void, and will automatically terminate your rights under this License. However, parties who have received copies, or rights, from you under this License will not have their licenses terminated so long as such parties remain in full compliance.

10. FUTURE REVISIONS OF THIS LICENSE

The Free Software Foundation may publish new, revised versions of the GNU Free Documentation License from time to time. Such new versions will be similar in spirit to the present version, but may differ in detail to address new problems or concerns. See http://www.gnu.org/copyleft/.

Each version of the License is given a distinguishing version number. If the Document specifies that a particular numbered version of this License "or any later version" applies to it, you have the option of following the terms and conditions either of that specified version or of any later version that has been published (not as a draft) by the Free Software Foundation. If the Document does not specify a version number of this License, you may choose any version ever published (not as a draft) by the Free Software Foundation.

ADDENDUM: How to use this License for your documents

To use this License in a document you have written, include a copy of the License in the document and put the following copyright and license notices just after the title page:

```
Copyright (C)  year  your name.
Permission is granted to copy, distribute and/or modify this document
under the terms of the GNU Free Documentation License, Version 1.2
or any later version published by the Free Software Foundation;
with no Invariant Sections, no Front-Cover Texts, and no Back-Cover
Texts.  A copy of the license is included in the section entitled ``GNU
Free Documentation License''.
```

If you have Invariant Sections, Front-Cover Texts and Back-Cover Texts, replace the "with. . . Texts." line with this:

```
with the Invariant Sections being list their titles, with
the Front-Cover Texts being list, and with the Back-Cover Texts
being list.
```

If you have Invariant Sections without Cover Texts, or some other combination of the three, merge those two alternatives to suit the situation.

If your document contains nontrivial examples of program code, we recommend releasing these examples in parallel under your choice of free software license, such as the GNU General Public License, to permit their use in free software.

OpenOCD Concept Index

X

Z

Command and Driver Index

www.ingramcontent.com/pod-product-compliance
Lightning Source LLC
LaVergne TN
LVHW060142070326
832902LV00018B/2908